Laughter In The Blue Mist

Dan C. Armstrong, Sr.

authorHOUSE®

AuthorHouse™
1663 Liberty Drive
Bloomington, IN 47403
www.authorhouse.com
Phone: 1-800-839-8640

First published by AuthorHouse 1/26/2010

ISBN: 978-1-4490-3663-8 (sc)

Printed in the United States of America
Bloomington, Indiana

This book is printed on acid-free paper.

DEDICATION

First, to my wife, Faith Dowdy Armstrong, who was my motivating force behind my writing this book. To my Mother and Father, Ruth Burkhart Armstrong and Darak Blackburn Armstrong who battled all the effects of the Depression while raising three children. Against all odds, they won.

ACKNOWLEDGEMENTS

Grateful thanks to my wife, Faith Dowdy Armstrong, for many hours of typing the manuscript and handling the business aspects of having the book published.

For reading and giving helpful evaluations of the early manuscripts:

Clint Armstrong, Carol Eason, Teresa Wallace – my three children

Ben Alig, O.D., Kingsport, Tennessee

Fred Jones, Scholar, Athens, Georgia

Hugh Morgan, Childhood friend since elementary school in Knoxville, Tennessee, now resides in Apopka, Florida

Charlotte and Robert McGeehee, Childhood friends in Knoxville, Tennessee, still reside in Knoxville

Thomas Naugle, Poet, Madison, Florida

Mary Powers, Kingsport, Tennessee

Dr. Dee Shelnutt, Methodist minister, former pastor in Fayetteville, Georgia, now pastor in Alpharetta, Georgia

Kathy Spence, Gainesville, Georgia

FOREWORD

There was a thin, blue mist of fear and sadness floating through the minds and hearts of everyone who lived in the time of the Great Depression.

Energy and ambition wandered with no place to go, lying limp in distress and hopelessness. It magnified the blue nature of our life.

Amid the generalized sadness that gripped our world —we had fun despite the crumbling world around us – and, there was laughter in the blue mist.

PREFACE

More than seventy-five years have passed since the Great Depression of the 1930's, but we are facing some of the same economic problems now in 2009: Stock market on the skids, massive employment, and shrinking real estate market. Some of the stories in this book will have an emotional feel akin to the era in which we live right now.

Dan C. Armstrong, Sr., D. Min.

TABLE OF CONTENTS

INTRODUCTION

The very word "Depression" is still a haunting word. We lost our home in Fountain City, a suburb of Knoxville, Tennessee. My Father was unemployed from the Southern Railway for eleven months, and I started to school in the first grade. My brother was four, and my sister, two.

These were bad times, but there were good times during the bad times. We came out of these distressing times much stronger, but forever scarred.

One of the most shameful, terminal effects of the 1930's on young people was the feeling of inferiority. There were so many indications that we were second-class. Not only blue-collar families, but also many white-collar families suffered humiliation. I remember seeing businessmen in expensive suits with the lapels and cuffs worn threadbare. Shirt collars and cuffs that had the first layer of cloth worn through and curled back were so commonplace that everyone expected it. When the shirts were washed, heavy starch was put in the collar to help paste down the frayed edges when ironed. This created a saw-edge that scraped a neck raw.

Shoes were always a disgrace. They were half-soled and rubber-heeled at home – rather than purchasing new shoes. The "dimestore" did a land-office business in do-it-yourself rubber soles. Two rubber soles came stapled on a cardboard card with glue and a bent piece of bright metal with a rough area like a grater. When the shoes were dry, we would rough-up the existing sole of the shoe, then put glue on both the old and new sole; let them dry slightly; and then stick them together. Seldom did we get them on exactly straight. Of course, there was always the fresh, warm cardboard in the shoe to plug up a hole on a rainy day. I remember coming home from school with my socks wet and feet cold. My Mother would cut a new cardboard innersole for my shoes and give me dry socks. I can still feel the warmth and comfort of fresh cardboard. It was more than physical. There was psychological warmth from Mother's love. It must have pained her terribly to see us in such ragged shoes.

There was no anger toward our parents because of our economic pain. We were in it together. The adversity brought us closer together and made us determined to overcome the great odds against us. I believe it helped us to value the individual with a greater understanding. No one could feel superior to someone else. We were all poor and needed and understood each other.

The Depression became a reality to our family when our Daddy was laid-off from the Southern Railway. Bad economic times were closing factories and businesses, and the railroad was no exception. Our Dad was a machinist. The shop was closed tighter than an iron gate; and the men, proud men, were turned out to wander the streets. I remember Dad getting up every morning and leaving as though he were going to work. He would return home in the late afternoon. He had always worked since he was seventeen years of age; and now, there was no work. What does a proud, able-bodied, skilled man do when there is no work? It was years later that I discovered that many of the railroad men, even though they were not working, retained their passes to ride the train for free. My Dad, along with many other men, from Southern Railway, would meet at the railroad station in the morning and catch a local train. (The locals stopped at little towns, along the line) The men would ride about fifty miles through the East Tennessee hills and return to Knoxville in the afternoon. Often, they would stop in various towns to seek work, but most of the little towns were in worse shape than our hometown. They rode the train to get off the streets. They did not want to look like unemployed bums – these were proud men.

For eleven straight months, the shops were closed. Our Dad found odd jobs here and there, but the sustaining grace for our family was a garden in the backyard, relatives with farms who had hogs and cows, and our good credit at a grocery store on Cedar Lane in Fountain City.

Before the Depression, our parents had bought a house on Charles Street in Fountain City (today a part of Knoxville). It was a newly-developed area, and houses were some distance apart. Our yard seemed quite large. In the backyard, we had a large garden plot and a chicken yard. They supplied us with some of our food needs.

Our Aunts and Uncles on Mother's side of the family, all lived on farms. When it was hog- killing time, Dad would help with the kill, and we shared in the bounty of sausage, livers, and various other hog parts.

We did not make a house payment for many months. The real estate company wanted to keep the house occupied, but we later did lose the house.

Our credit at the grocery store was God-sent. We charged groceries for the full eleven months never paying a cent during that period. My Dad and Mother began to pay small amounts after my Dad went back to work for a few hours per week. It was not until my Dad received his WWI Bonus in 1936 that we paid the bulk of the bill.

We had moved to 1150 Eleanor Street in Knoxville. The whole family sat on the front porch the day the postman was delivering the Bonus Checks. This was a special mail delivery. The postman came in the afternoon and was delivering only the Bonus Checks. We sat waiting, as he criss-crossed the street, having each recipient to sign for the delivery. My brother, sister and I would sneak off the porch to peer up the street to check on the postman's progress. We would hurry back to the porch to announce to our parents just how many houses were between us and the postman. He was not stopping at every house – just the houses of veterans. We felt very proud and special to know that the postman would stop at our house. For kids who felt very unspecial and rather low on the economic scale, the postman's stopping that day at *our* house was a very big event.

We watched our Dad as he signed for his check; and we listened to the crisp rattle of the official, brown government envelope, as he carefully and slowly opened it. We stared in amazement at the official U.S. Government check. We had never seen so much money. We felt very rich, with more than $600 when the average yearly income was $1,500.

The next day the check was cashed, and the whole family made the pilgrimage to the grocery store. This was an old-style store with a gas pump out front with a large glass container on top showing the reddish gasoline. The floor of the store was black from oil used to keep the dust down. A large glass counter surrounded the center area around the cash register. Open baskets of vegetables lined the floor.

In the back was a cabinet where the individual purchase tickets were kept. The grocer, in a long, white apron, greeted my Dad. We stood in a silent line as our Dad stated that we had come to pay our bill. He opened the cabinet and produced a very large stack of tickets. In the top ticket was the eleven-month balance of nearly $350. We watched while our Dad counted out the money. My brother, sister and I were eyeing the candy counter. It was the custom to give a sack of candy to the kids when the grocery bill was paid. The grocer was more than faithful to the custom. He filled a very large bag with a variety of candy. It was so full that stick candy was protruding from the top of the bag.

I remember my Mother and Dad thanking the grocer for his faith in them. He said that he never doubted that the bill would be paid.

I felt very proud to come from the kind of people who were trusted and always paid their bills.

On the way home, Lynn, Martha, and I sat on the backseat of the car, eating our candy. The roaring motor of the Hupmobile drowned out most conversation. We knew that we had been freed of a great debt. We were very content, humming in concert with the vibrations and motor noise of our Grandfather's 1929 automobile. Looking back on the Depression years, I recall that we laughed a lot. I am astonished when I hear that kids of today cannot cope in the high-stress modern society. I can understand stress, fear, being poor, living in a blue world, surrounded by what seemed to be endless hopelessness. But, none of those things are as great today as they were in the 1930's.

The 1930's were a time of humiliation, following on the heels of the great expectations of the 1920's. Everything was lost for the average person. For ten or eleven years, there was a constant struggle for survival.

A generalized sadness gripped our world. There was no place to turn – no place to get help. But – there was laughter, and we had fun despite the crumbling world around us.

CHAPTER 1

CHRISTMAS AT HOME

FOR MY BROTHER, SISTER AND ME, there always seemed to be an abundance at Christmastime – even in the lean and bleak years.

The winters in the 1930's were rather severe with chilling cold and wind-blown snow. It seemed just another insult to the human spirit struggling for survival.

Daddy would often stand at the window and stare out at the cold outside. It reflected much of the chill he felt inside his soul. He had never been jobless before, and he was a responsible man.

Christmas always had a continuity. The decorations, used year-after-year, had a code of happiness of their own. The window wreaths and tree ornaments were old friends. When Mother pulled the worn boxes from their storage place in the attic, a new joy began to ring through the house. Daddy would put the wooden stand on the tree bottom, while Mother unpacked the familiar decorations and began selecting the proper wreaths and bells for each location in the house. They were rather simple things that we had had for years. Their emotional value was so much more than their dollar cost. They created new life of brightness and joy in an otherwise gray and depressed world.

Christmas 1930 was especially cold, with snow filling our driveway waist-deep to a six-year old boy. The whole landscape was covered in a blanket of white. We were looking for Santa Claus to bring a bountiful collection of toys and goodies.

It was a great Christmas with toys, clothes, candy and nuts. The house was warm and decorated with red and green.

I remember well the mechanical steam-shovel, the warm gloves with a cuff, a leather aviator's cap with long ear-flaps, crayons, and a metal box full of colored marbles.

Mother baked a turkey and made the most delicious dressing to be covered with her special gravy. There were pies and cakes and boiled custard.

The candy dishes were full, and there were apples, oranges, dates, and extra-large raisins. The whole house was like a fairyland of good things.

The painful secret of this wonderful Christmas was not known until I was grown. My Dad told me that he had borrowed $100 from a "loan-shark" – the only one that would loan an unemployed railroad man money. Daddy paid him in $5.00 and $10.00 payments for nearly three years. When he could not pay, he was threatened and had more interest added to the original principal. The shark's goons would harass him, often when he was on the street downtown, but my Dad knew how they operated when he borrowed the money. He was determined to have Christmas for his three young children – six, four, and two year's old who believed in Santa Claus. It took a lot of courage.

CHAPTER 2

OUR FATHER

My Father was not the favorite child. His fat sister was the chosen one. His life was a constant struggle to be "blessed". As far as I could tell, he never received that which he sought.

He was born four years from the turn-of-the 20th Century. His sister was his senior by two years.

His childhood years were the years of no child labor laws. This allowed him to start work at a very early age – working after school and on weekends. He worked in a trunk factory. He often told of excessive heat and noise, mixing in the foul air of industrial progress. He moved heavy trunks on his back and stacked them for display. When he was older, he carried both the morning and evening paper to support himself. He paid his parents for his room and meals.

His superior athletic ability was cut short because of his extensive work schedule. But, even against these odds that prevented him from playing football and baseball in high school, he became a star baseball pitcher when he left school in the eleventh grade to work for Southern Railway. He played on the railroad team, but was often allowed to pitch for other teams. One of his friends told me that when he pitched, he usually won. He could throw a "smoking" fast ball.

After his death, I found a small newspaper clipping, yellowed with age, in an old billfold. It stated:

> Darak B. Armstrong pitched the Southern Railway Baseball Team to victory with his blazing fast ball. He allowed only two hits. Southern Railway –3; Standard – 0

He must have saved this small bit of history all those years as a testimony to what he could have been. He started work at the railroad when he was seventeen as a machinist[1] apprentice and retired after forty-five years. He kept the job that he hated because of security and good retirement. He really liked the out-of-doors and wanted to be a Forest Ranger. He loved animals and plants of all types. I believe that he would have lived a calmer and happier life if he could have been surrounded with woodland, birds, and animals.

The spirit of adventure had long been drummed out of him by the excessive desire to be accepted. He worked hard and in excess to claim his right to be loved and accepted by his parents. The unaccepting response was reflected in his anxious and nervous nature. He showed an inferiority complex as he attempted to challenge the world. He never accepted opportunities for promotion.

Being a foreman would have put him in a superior position to the men – and they would not have liked him. "Everyone hates the boss." To be the superior person, as he saw his parents, always meant being an abuser who could never be pleased, and who was hated by everyone. He never wanted that role. He never took a promotion at the railroad.

---

[1] A railroad machinist is a person trained for years to become a Journeyman who has detailed knowledge of both steam, electric, and diesel railroad engines. They are capable of making minor or major overhauls of the giant engines, keeping them running uninterrupted at a safe and rapid speed as they pull passenger cars or a hundred or more boxcars or coal cars over great distances.

As a Father, he wanted us to be model children – children that followed the rules – and did nothing to embarrass him. Our greatest punishment came when our actions reflected on his role as a Father and disciplinarian. I once climbed up a mound of sand and lime at a building site of a new house. The man next door yelled at me, and my Dad over-heard the noise. He rushed from the house and spanked me severely. As I see it now, there was a danger in my damaging my eyes in the lime. I was, however, punished for violating his code of ethics. No concern was given to why a young kid wanted to climb a seemingly inert pile of sand with white stuff in it.

I recycled the emotional trauma by trying to earn his love. He never knew how to be very close or speak about sensitive things like love or affection. He always wanted to appear as a tough and rugged person showing his well-developed arms and chest. It was a bluff. He was basically a very sensitive man in love with the natural world. He was hard to know because he protected his sensitive nature. He talked rough, but not vulgar. He walked with a swagger. He was a proud man. He had to ware bib overalls when he was working in the railroad shop, but I never saw him wear them because each day, when he finished work, he would wash his face and hands to remove the grease and grime and change into khaki pants and shirt to wear home. He dressed well when it was a dress-up occasion – for church or business downtown. He always wore a hat with his three-piece suit. There was never a wrinkle in his clothes nor a scuff on his shoes. He was a handsome man. He did not like being identified as a blue-collar worker because, in his heart, he was not.

I was always proud of him, but I never told him.

Our closest and most sensitive moment came about two weeks before his death. He had a stroke, and I came from Atlanta to Knoxville to see him. While I was there, he grew worse and was hospitalized. It was a few days before Christmas, and I was going back to Atlanta to be with my family for the holidays. I was saying good-bye to him in his hospital room. "I am going home for a few days, but I will return about New

5

Year's Day. Will you be okay?" He replied in a weak, high-pitched voice, "I will be okay, but I will feel a little less secure with you gone."

Those words still haunt me because I left that day, and my Father died a few days later. We had said our last words.

It could have been the greatest moment in our lives to be close. I could have told him that I loved him and how proud I was for all the things that he had accomplished in his life. I miss him more as each year goes by, and I understand him more because I am his son. I have his temperament, and I try to live and do those things that my Father never had the opportunity to enjoy. I am okay, but I feel a little less secure with him gone.

CHAPTER 3

OUR MOTHER

IN THE TOTAL SCHEME OF THINGS, women in history seldom get the recognition they deserve for their sacrifices and heroism. I hereby inscribed these words to note that our Mother was truly a heroine. Throughout the Depression, she was a stabilizing force in our family that kept us on an even keel in the most difficult times. She always had an answer or solution to some of the most hopeless problems. She was always stable and had the ability to develop a plan that gave direction when we were floundering in a seemingly hopeless situation. When our Dad was at his wits' end and nervously paced the floor while dealing with endless impasses, Mother would put her arm around him, and they would talk quietly. Dad would settle down and suddenly find an answer.

Mother was born Mary Ruth Burkhart in 1899 in Knox County, Tennessee, in the Asbury community. She was the third of seven children: five girls and two boys. Her Father was a farmer. My Mother milked cows before school and drove a team of horses several miles to attend high school. She never liked the farm. She was a liberated woman before the words were coined. After high school, she moved to Knoxville and lived with her Grandmother and worked in the office of Swann's Bakery on Magnolia Avenue. She learned to drive a car before most men her age and later taught my Father to drive.

She and Dad were married in 1921. They had their first child two years later, a girl. She lived only a few hours. For years, Mother would cry for her lost child. I think it made her more sensitive to all of life.

Mother extruded an attitude of confidence. To the challenge of: "You can't", her blue eyes would twinkle, and she would reply, "I can."

She always stood on "tiptoes of expectation" and saw beauty in the most basic things in life. She would excite us all when we would discover a small flower along the walk. "Isn't that the most beautiful flower you have ever seen." It wasn't uncommon for her to express her delight in a well-prepared meal with, 'I believe these are the best rolls I have ever eaten." She helped us to be aware that we were surrounded by good and beautiful things.

Most women worked in the home, but in the mid-1930's, my Mother felt that she would break custom and find herself a job. There were many things that we needed, and Dad was working only three or four days a week at the railroad. Much to Daddy's chagrin, Mother found a political job at the County Courthouse in the Trustee's office. She had always been active in politics and worked for various candidates at election time. Our Dad reminded her that political jobs were not reliable because she would lose her job with the fate of her candidate. Out Mother was a politician at heart, however, and kept her job for forty years through various Democrat and Republican office holder.

Mother had strong opinions, but she never imposed her will on her children. She let us make our own mistakes but protected us like a lioness.

When I was twelve years old, I had a paper route. Several of the subscribers would not pay me the money they owed. Mother couldn't take it too long, and she would go to the person and say, "I know you have just forgotten to pay my son for the last three weeks." They would usually apologize and cough-up the money. There was one man on my route who sat on the front porch in his undershirt in the hot summer months. When I passed his house, he would stand up and say, "Hey boy, give me a paper, or I will come out there and git one." I gave him a paper every day. My Mother heard about this and followed me one afternoon. After I gave the man the paper, my Mother followed within a few minutes. She walked up on the porch and snatched the paper from the surprised man. "Don't you ever threaten my son again." He never did. In fact, when I came down the street delivering the paper, he usually got up and went inside the house.

Her compassion equaled her determination to see the right prevail. During the leanest years of the Depression, people often came to the door requesting a bite to eat. Our Mother never just gave a bite to eat. She prepared a full meal and served it on a tray with a doily under the plate and a cloth napkin.

Women appear to be fragile and need to be protected. It might be said another way. They are delicate like fine china but represent the supreme accomplishment of creation.

Our Mother lived to be 93 years old.

CHAPTER 4

OUR GRANDFATHER – NaNa
(Our Father's Father)

My Grandfather, John Blackburn Armstrong, had a small farm in Redhouse, Tennessee. In 1920, he sold his small farm for a slightly larger and more picturesque location between two mountains in Joppa, Tennessee. He loved to farm. My Grandmother liked to live in town. She had some exaggerated idea that to live on a farm was low-class. So, they lived in town in a big two-story house and would go to the farm in the Summer on weekends and sometimes for a two or three- week stay.

My Great-great-great Grandfather was given a land grant of some 1,000 acres of bottomland at the end of the Revolutionary War. My Great-grandfather later divided the huge farm between his eight children. My Grandfather's share was about 150 acres. NaNa could have spent his life there, living close to the soil. He loved the freedom of being near nature. He liked to hear the wind in the trees and could sense a summer shower hours before it arrived. He could sit for hours in the woods being refreshed by the sounds of the birds and the bark of a fox. He sold the land he loved so much and settled for his small plot of land in the county and house in the city. My Grandmother would not live off the hard-surface road, nor anywhere else, with much happiness.

NaNa worked for Southern Railway for a number of years on the wrecking crew. He was called when there was a train wreck or a derailment. This was very dirty and dangerous work. To please my Grandmother, he left the railroad and became a city policeman in Knoxville. He was 6'2", 290 lbs. and made an impressive sight in his stovepipe policeman's hat and his ankle-length uniform coat. His police badge was as large as a lard can lid. His hands were huge. Someone said he looked as if he were carrying sugar-cured hams.

I have read stories of his exploits as a policeman. He and two other very large men were the Riot Squad. Their total weight was near 1,000 lbs. My Dad told me that rarely did they need to rough-up anyone. The very sight of them often would quell a bar fight.

Once the three were called because of a pay-day riot in a bar on Depot Street. Men were drunk, throwing chairs and beer mugs, turning over tables. The Riot Squad arrived. They cast a shadow over the whole room, as they stood, holding their nightsticks across their chests. There was a sudden hush over the bar. Men began to put tables and chairs upright, brush broken glass into neat little piles, and some even mopped the spilled beer from the floor. Soon, everyone was seated and quiet. My Grandfather and his two companions had not moved from their position. They turned and quietly filed out into the dimness of the gas-lighted street, without saying a word to anyone.

On another occasion, my Grandfather went out alone and subdued three men attempting to steal horses. He caught them in a barn putting the bridle and saddle on two thoroughbreds. One pulled a Barlow knife and made a move toward my Grandfather and was immediately dispatched with a backhand slash of his nightstick. He chased the other two. (He was unusually fast for a big man) and collared them rather quickly. He was returning to the station, standing on the back of the horse-drawn paddy wagon, when the wagon flipped over, crushing his right hand.

He was rushed to the M.D.'s office by six policemen, only to hear that the doctor planned to amputate his hand. My Grandfather stood and slowly looked around the room, and then, at the doctor, "I don't believe there are enough men in the room to take off my hand." With these words, he folded a towel over his crushed hand and walked home. After many months of treatment with herb drinks and home-made topical applications, his hand was healed. When I knew him many years later, his hand was in perfect working order. He never trusted doctors, nor did he ever go to another, trusting only in his own home remedies. He used Aspirin, home-made liniment, and laxatives, along with his secret herbs.

He retired from the Knoxville Police Department several years later and lived to be 87 years old. He received a pension of $60 per month.

CHAPTER 5

OUR GRANDMOTHER (MaMaw)
(Our Father's Mother)

SHE WASN'T AN EASY PERSON TO love. She revealed a soured-on-the-world attitude. She constantly complained of headaches, upset stomach, and a "swimmy head". We always thought that she just complained to get attention. We didn't give it a second thought, but she might have really been sick. It couldn't have been very serious. She lived to be 96, outliving her husband by eleven years.

We never visited her without receiving a tea cake. It was no ordinary round cookie. It melted in our mouths. She always used plenty of country butter and Watkin's real vanilla. Her pound cakes were equally delicious with a pound of country butter, a dozen eggs, plus the vanilla.

She loved flowers. Her yard and large round porch were always covered with plants. Moss-lined wire baskets were the home for her favorite – begonias. When she worked in her flowers, she dressed as any Southern woman should. She always protected herself from the sun with long gloves and a wide-brimmed straw hat. She abhorred the idea of having freckles and darkness on her cream-colored skin. It was not the mark of a Southern lady.

She was never on time. We always had to wait for her to get ready to go anywhere. Our Grandfather would be in the car with the motor warmed-up at least thirty minutes before Mamaw made her appearance. She would slowly amble out of the house, observing her flowers and touching the new blooms. She always dusted her face with Cody powder, never removing her glasses. She appeared as though she had just passed through a snowstorm, with her glasses still glazed with the evidence. She would enter the car, complaining that she needed to have her glasses changed – everything looked hazy.

She could wake in the morning with a "sick headache", go to downtown Knoxville at 10:00 a.m. and shop nonstop until 4:30 p.m., and never show signs of tiring. She and her daughter, Aunt Leta, would tell our Grandfather to meet them on Gay Street in front of S.H. George and Sons Department Store at 1:00 p.m. He would sit there, patiently for three-and-a-half hours. He did have a problem with his kidneys and would need to relieve himself two or three times during the wait. He understood well the dimensions of the wait, so he developed a convenient system to prevent the frequent trip into the department store toilet. He rigged a metal funnel on the end of three feet of rubber hose that extended through the floorboard of the car. It always worked well. He held the funnel between his legs with a newspaper in his lap. It offered all the privacy of being at home.

One day, after a several-hour wait, a friend came by and spoke to our Grandfather. After a short conversation, the man jumped back and looked under the car. "My God, Uncle John, I believe your car has sprung a leak." The man crawled under the car, sniffing the liquid on the ground. He put his hand in a small puddle, sniffed, and tasted it, with a sudden realization as to that the liquid was. He jumped to his feet, brushing his hands together and said, "See you later, Uncle John."

From time to time in the summer, Mamaw would go to McMinnville, Tennessee to visit her daughter. Our Uncle and Aunt would come to Knoxville and take Mamaw for the two-week or so visit. We lived a half a block down the hill on Eleanor Street, and we could see them loading the car and leaving. About ten minutes after their departure, NaNa would come down the front steps with his hat on, get in his car and leave. About a half-an-hour later, he would return. Even as children, we knew the ritual. He was making his pilgrimage to the bootlegger for his pint of refreshment while his wife was gone. He never drank when she was home. When we visited him each day while she was gone, he never seemed happier and would entertain us with one tall tale after another.

In reality, Mamaw was a rather sophisticated woman, with the poise from an age past. She must have dreamed of being pampered more and living a life with carriages and footmen and dashing young men, racing on horseback to rescue her when in distress. Her house was furnished with beautiful furniture, elegant tables, lamps with painted glass shades, and large palm plants to brighten the rooms.

She had a poise and grace that softened the hardness of life in the 1930's.

CHAPTER 6

NANA'S HUPMOBILE AND THE GRAY

It was a heavily-built auto – a 1927 Hupmobile. It sat high off the street with wooden spoked wheels and a spare tie on the rear of the car – grooved rubber on the wide running boards. It was originally black, but my Father and Mother, along with my Grandfather, decided to repaint it a dark green. After all, a car with color other than black was quite unusual in those days. They sanded the car from bumper-to-bumper, and painted the body with paintbrushes. It did look good, but I doubt if it would stand close inspection compare to today's spray and bake jobs.

The insides were quite fancy with bud vases on each side between the doors. The windshield would roll up about three inches to allow a flow of air on hot days.

The steering wheel was a massive wooden wheel. In the center was what looked like a stack of hotcakes with little levers ticking out of each one. The stack was capped with the horn button, which NaNa used a lot with its "uuga-uuga" sound. One of the levers on the "hotcake" stack was a throttle. NaNa had a problem with arthritis that inhibited any quick leg movements, so he would have the break and clutch depressed and used the throttle to increase the motor speed. He would then ease off the two pedals, and the car would move forward with a roar. My Father always said that it sounded like a threshing machine.

Automobiles were not that commonplace back when NaNa first learned to drive. He bought an automobile called a Gray in about 1919. One of the problems with some of these early cars was with the tires. Sometimes they just wouldn't stay on the rim. NaNa had this problem with his Gray. Soon after my Mother and Father were married, NaNa and my Grandmother, MaMaw, took them to their small mountain farm in Redhouse, Tennessee. On the return trip, the tires kept jumping the rims and rolling down the highway. After about three stops to retrieve and remount the tires, NaNa's Scots-Irish temper got the best of him, and he took all four tires off and came back into town on the rims. It was quite noisy, but they did well until they ran onto the streetcar tracks on Magnolia Avenue. There was nothing he could do. The flanges on the rims gripped the tracks. He couldn't turn left or right. He could only follow the tracks. He traveled several miles on into downtown Knoxville and then followed the tracks into the car barn at the end of Gay Street, across from the Courthouse. It was there that the workmen pried the Gray off the tracks, and helped NaNa get his tires back on the rims and sent him on his way home.

It was sometime later that the Hupmobile came into the family. One criteria he used to determine the suitability of his new auto was whether the tires would stay on the rims. He had no problem with the Hupmobile.

CHAPTER 7 ˙

A TRIP TO JOPPA IN THE HUPMOBILE

LYNN AND I USUALLY WENT EVERYWHERE together, but on this trip in 1938, Lynn went alone with my Grandfather and Grandmother to Joppa, Tennessee. The plan was that they would go up on one weekend and return the next. They packed the car with supplies for the week. NaNa always carried a pick and a shovel, a saw and an ax along on the trip. The Granger County Highway was a two-lane concrete highway, but at Joppa, he turned onto a gravel road that went up the mountain. Then, there came the left turn onto a sandy road that easily washed out and often had fallen trees across it.

NaNa's car was the only car that went down the road, so he had to repair the road as he went. Most people there rode horses or walked.

Our Grandparents' house was unique. It had a wooden shingled roof and wide, unpainted boards on the outside with a rock chimney. There were two large rooms: one was the kitchen and eating area and the other, the front room, served as their bedroom and sitting area. There were two other small side rooms: one was where guests slept, and the other was used for storage.

The most outstanding aspect of the house was the two huge oak trees that stood on each side of the front walk. It would take three men to reach around the trunks of the trees. The trees must have stood more than one hundred feet high. They shaded the whole house and

21

gave the house a character of its own. I could stand under the trees during a rain and play and never get wet.

It was early morning when my brother was packed and ready to go to the farm. We had a suitcase my Father always called "a grip" that we used for any trip. Our Mother had packed everything my brother would need for the week. They left with a roar up Eleanor Street hill, and they were on their way. Our Grandmother always took several things to eat for herself. She had a quart of milk, cookies and crackers. She never shared.

Our Grandfather always made one stop on the 30 mile trip to get a Coke and a snack. Our grandmother could not drink carbonated beverages. She also couldn't drink from a bottle, so she always brought along a tin cup from which to drink her milk in style.

Lynn told me the story of what happened on this trip.

They were roaring along the concrete highway. MaMaw was drinking her milk from the tin cup and munching a cracker when NaNa missed a curve, and the Hupmobile left the road. It went down an embankment and through a barbed-wire fence. He still had the gas peddle depressed as the car roared through a cornfield, dragging 20 feet of barbed wire and two fence posts, cutting a swath through 10 foot corn. It was like going through water. No one could see anything but corn ahead and to each side. Suddenly, they broke out of the corn into the open as our Grandfather was still holding his foot on the accelerator. He circled the barn where an astonished farmer stood watching. Then, NaNa plunged back into the cornfield towards the highway. The cornfield opened again like the water for Moses through the Red Sea. He drove back through the barbed-wire fence. Suddenly, NaNa hit the brakes, and the car skidded sideways. The side of the car leaned up against the incline leading to the highway.

There was a moment of silence, broken by MaMaw in an angry tone, "John, you made me spill my milk!" She was totally unaware that they had ever left the hard surface road.

Later, during the week, Lynn decided that there was some urgent business that he had to attend to at home and couldn't wait for the return trip. He went to Hammer's General Store in Joppa and caught the Greyhound Bus home.

CHAPTER 8

EXCESSES

OUR DAD WORKED ON THE THEORY that: "If a little does good, a lot more would be much better."

Early one summer, he had the urge to have a nice stand of grass on our very small front yard which was about fifty feet wide.

He splurged and purchased a 50 lb. Bag of fertilizer. The directions said to use about a quart on each side of the center walk. He used about a quart and a half on each side.

Each evening, he would sit on the screened front porch waiting for nature's miracle of lush green grass.

After two weeks, we noticed a slight greening of the existing grass but no sudden surge of growth. One evening, Dad had taken all the slow growth he could handle. He scattered the remainder of the 50 pounds of fertilizer. The yard was white. We were sitting on the porch when Mother came out of the house. In her dry, pointed wit, she said, 'Well, it looks like we have had a summer snowfall."

We spent the summer of 1938 looking at a front yard as bare as a baseball infield – not one sprig of grass.

Dad was seldom sick, but one cold, winter afternoon, he came home from work with a cold, sore throat and aches and pains. He ate supper and took a very hot bath and drank a large glass of baking soda and water.

Then, the capstone of the treatment – Sloane's Liniment – the hottest and most powerful liniment on the drugstore shelf. The instructions said not to rub it in, but to pat in on "sparingly".

Dad rubbed it on his neck real good. Our Mother cautioned him not to rub it in, but . . ."If a little does well, a lot is better". So, he splashed it on generously and rubbed and rubbed.

He was in bed about a half-hour when we heard him jump out of bed and run into the bathroom. His neck was as red as a turkey gobbler. He stuck his head and neck under the faucet in the bathtub and ran cold water over his head and neck.

As my brother, Lynn, and I were going to bed, we passed Dad sitting in the living room – neck, glowing red. Lynn looked at Dad, and then at me, and said, "Gobble, Gobble", as we got out of hearing distance.

CHAPTER 9

THE ELECTRIC REFRIGERATOR AND STOVE

PRIOR TO CHEAP ELECTRICITY FROM THE TVA, we had an oil cook stove and an icebox.

The oil stove was of rather fragile construction. It stood on delicate legs with two cooking eyes, and the small oven was on the right side, sitting over the two remaining units. The burner in each eye had a woven wick that soaked up kerosene. When lighted, it provided the heat on which to cook. The kerosene was on the left of the stove in a glass container that had to be inverted so the valve on the cap would allow a small amount of kerosene to dribble out and through small pipes to the various eyes.

It was impossible to fill the glass container without getting the smell of kerosene on your clothes.

Most people had a one-gallon can to bring oil from the store. They would get the can filled, and the groceryman would stick a potato on the spout to prevent it from spilling.

My Dad felt that carrying that small can to the store every week and returning with a potato stuck on the spout was tacky. So, we had a five-gallon can with a screw-on cap on the spout. On one trip to the store, the grocery man, Mr. Buffett, dropped the spout cap and rather than look for it, he just stuck a potato on the spout. When I arrived home, I thought my Dad would have a stroke. "We look like common trash with a potato stock on our oil can." I had to rush back to the store and scrounge around under the oil tank to find the cap and to once again, restore our oilcan's dignity. We could, again, carry oil from the store with poise and grace and with no potato.

The Tennessee Valley Authority (TVA) was organized in 1933, and soon after that time, the Norris Dam was constructed, primarily to control the annual flooding in the Tennessee Valley. But, the production of electricity and super phosphate were the two major factors directly affecting the people and the land. The super phosphate helped to green the land and produce better food crops. The cheap electricity helped people to come out of a retarded age and made affordable more modern electric appliances.

I remember when we first purchased a new Frigidaire and an electric stove to replace the icebox and oil stove. When we had company, they always had to come to the kitchen to see our new stuff. My Mother was very happy. She personified the two machines as she caressed them while she told neighbors about how great it was to have such modern appliances.

We thought it very special to have ice cream made in the ice tray. This was the modern way. Our ice tray was special. To avoid arguments as to who had the most ice cream, our Dad measured the tray into five equal sections and marked them. For years, later on, you could still see the cut marks in the bottom of the tray where the five equal sections were divided. This may well be a symbol of our family. Everything was divided as equally as possible. None of us felt that we had to fight for our part in anything. What we received was our equal part – without question. It was a rude awakening to find that the rest of the world wasn't that way. But it did give "home" a special meaning. When we removed the old icebox and replaced it with the modern electric refrigerator, the historical past began to fade away.

Before the electric refrigerator, the ice sign was a part of every household. It was placed in the window or door so the iceman could see it from the street. It was turned to indicate how much ice was needed. On each of the four sides of the sign was "25-50-75-100". This stood for the number of pounds of ice that the household wanted to buy. It cost 10 cents for each 25 lbs. Even the buying of ice had its social impact. There were those who would buy 100 lbs. at a time. This was to let the world know that they were affluent and could afford the best. Most people bought 25-50 lbs.

We had a nosey neighbor who strolled down the street on ice day just to check ice signs to see how much ice the people were buying. My Mother hated such tactics, so to counter the neighbor, Mother would turn our sign to 100 lbs. until the nosey neighbor had passed, and then she would return it to the 25 or 50 lbs. she wanted.

On hot summer days, we would sit on the curb waiting for the horse-drawn Morgan Co. Ice Wagon to appear. It was a large-wheeled covered wagon with a step on the back. The ice came in 300 lb. Blocks, and the iceman would chip out with an ice pick the size needed for each house. This meant a lot of ice chips in the wagon. We would follow the wagon two or three blocks, eating ice and riding on the step.

All horses had names, so the iceman would just holler, "Okay, Sam (or Charlie) – move it up a bit." And the horses would walk to the next house and would stop on command. "That's good – -hold it right there."

Icemen were always wet, from carrying ice. But the most noticeable aspect of their job was that they always had their pockets full of change. They would jingle when they walked and would have a handful of money to give change. When I was a kid, I always wanted to be as rich as an iceman.

CHAPTER 10

RELIGIOUS EXPERIENCE

THE LARGE DOMED LIGHTS WERE TOO mellow to well light the church sanctuary, but it was light enough to expose the frayed fullness of the carpet and the appearance of the people gathered for the annual night gathering for a week of preaching by a visiting evangelist, brought in to revive the congregation of the First Cumberland Presbyterian Church.

I was five years old and hated this type of religious service. My reason for being here with my Mother was the hope of getting an ice cream cone at the Courtesy Drug Store on the corner of Broadway and Fifth Avenue when this awful meeting was over.

The church gradually filled with mostly older people. They were familiar faces I had known most of my short life. I was baptized in this church as an infant. My Father had been a member since a child. My Mother joined when they were married. My Grandfather and Grandmother were active members for 40 years. My Uncle Walter Carter was a Charter Member. He was in his late 80's. The church was a comfortable place for me. I felt it had history for me and my family.

There was a calmness as the people came in, and the organist played a hymn for mood music. A man and his wife came in and sat in the pew in front of us. She was rather wide in the hips, and the bright dress didn't help in hiding that fact. He was well-dressed in a suit and tie, and he carried his hat. As he sat down, he saw me and winked and gave me a friendly smile. She came most every Sunday, but he came only on special occasions. But, he was a very good man. He always took time to recognize children. He had a genuine and sincere attitude. There was nothing phony about him – children have that special ability to understand feelings. This, of course, is drummed out of us long before we reach adulthood.

The service proceeded through the usual emotional hymns and a few testimonies, followed by a show-biz sermon. Then the *coup d'etat* – the scalp-count that determined whether the service was a success.

As we stood for the last hymn, the emotional request was made to have all sinners come forward. I was dreaming of a double-dip ice cream and wanted this to be over as soon as possible. Of course, one stanza wasn't enough, since those coming forward were rather sparse. Another and another stanza was sung. Then, it became "serious". Individuals appointed themselves to "save" those whom they felt were lost.

Suddenly, a man appeared beside the gentleman in front of me. This "saint" was pleading with him and talking about the "fires of Hell". He began to pray in a loud voice for God to save this man from eternal damnation. My friend was becoming uncomfortable. Another "saint" replaced the first and tried to pull my friend down the aisle. Then, they asked him to sit down. This is where I got close to the action. As I stood behind their pew, my head was between them at eye level. I could hear everything that was said. My friend kept saying, "No"; and the "saint" tried every type of manipulation from "sin" to the "Pearly Gates". I listened to one, then the other, and I felt this was pure Hell. How could any honorable person treat another person like this in the name of God's love?

I remember I put my hand lightly on my friend's shoulder to defend him from this vicious attack, but it was to no avail. Others came, until, finally, he jumped to his feet and stomped down to the front to shake the evangelist's hand. He had the look of "What the Hell! I'll be here all night if I don't go forward."

I felt that there had been a great conspiracy between some of the church members and my friend's wife to get him to church that night so that the "big guns" could attack and get him "saved". I felt it to be dishonorable and unfair and generally unethical. I hated what they had done to him. There was, of course, great rejoicing. Many people gathered to congratulate him on being "saved".

As we filed out of the church, I was deep in thought about this emotional experience and was unusually quiet. Mother talked with various people and shook the pastor's hand as we left. We caught a streetcar and went home. It was the next day that I remembered the ice cream cone.

I never saw my friend at church again. I will always miss him.

CHAPTER 11

THE MAPLE TREE CAPER

EVEN THOUGH THE JULY TEMPERATURE IN the sun was in the 90's, there was a cool breeze under the shade of the large silver maple tree.

Lynn, my brother, and I were enjoying the shade and telling tall tales trying to cause the other to laugh. The tree was sort of a home-base for talking and planning on a summer day. It was an easy tree to climb, and we would often shinny up to the very top for complete solitude. We could look down on the whole neighborhood and hear and see everyone's business without being observed.

Already that morning, Lynn and I had had a contest to see who could hang from a tree limb the longest while the other was saying funny words. Lynn won. I was hanging there, full of confidence, with my hands locked on the limb; and he was reeling off a string of words to get me off the limb: "sour grass", "grasshopper", "banana split", "white house" --- "House -----shoe". That was it. I lost my grip and fell in a heap and laughed until tears ran down my face. We lay on our backs, looking up into the mass of green leaves moving in the breeze. Gradually, the intense laughter began to subside, and we rested quietly for a while as we made plans for our next activity.

Anytime now, we expected to be interrupted by Fatso, who lived next door. He weighed twenty or thirty pounds more than us and used his weight to bully us around. But, like most bullies, he was easy to out-maneuver and trap.   Lynn and I had found a discarded trunk in the alley a few weeks before. We removed the curved trunk lid and tied a rope securely around the body of the trunk. We tied the other end around a strong limb, high in the tree, taut enough to just lift the trunk off the ground.

Our plan was to twist the trunk round and round, kinking the rope further and further up the tree. When the trunk was high enough, we were going to ride the trunk down to the ground again. That was the plan.

We twisted the trunk for a good hour and a half before the trunk finally reached the tree limb about twenty feet off the ground. The rope was a mass of knots. As we observed the situation from high in the tree, we had a growing concern about the whirling effect of the long ride to the ground. The distance to the ground seemed to be further and further, and our confidence for the ride began to wane.

As fate would have it, Fatso came out the back door of his house and hurried across the yard. He climbed the tree with great haste and said, "What are you doing?" I replied with great confidence, "We have been riding this trunk." Then Lynn said, with authority, "And, it's my turn!" As Lynn made a slight move toward the trunk, Fatso pushed him aside and hastily climbed into the trunk.

With a smile on our faces, we gave it a quick whirl and hurried down the tree.

The trunk started to whirl slowly. Fatso was sitting erect in the trunk with his arms stretched out along the top edge as though he were the King of the Universe. The whirling-speed increased, and we could hear a humm . . . humm . . .humm began as the trunk's speed became faster and faster. Fatso became a blur, and he gradually disappeared from view as he slipped into the floor of the trunk. We could not see him, but we could hear his moan.

It seemed like an eternity before the ride ended with Fatso throwing-up in the trunk. He mumbled something as he fell out of the trunk and crawled and staggered toward his house.

I said to Lynn, "I do not recall seeing Fatso that shade of green before."

We did not see him again for several days.

Lynn climbed the tree and untied the rope. With a grin in his voice, he said, "Well, what else can we use a trunk for?"

CHAPTER 12

THE BATTLE AT BIG RIDGE

BIG RIDGE STATE PARK WAS CRADLED in the hill-and-valley region of East Tennessee. A huge lake for swimming and boating was surrounded by hills covered with massive trees, hiking trails and rustic cabins with screened porches overlooking the lake.

When a group was planning an outing in the summer, they would, sooner or later, select Big Ridge State Park.

The road leading to the park had the appearance and contour of the Burma Road. It curved and zig-zagged up the side of a mountain before cresting and then plunging down the other side. It was on this road that we city boys learned a lesson from the country boys who lived in the mountains.

It was a hot, July Saturday, and we had been on a hay ride and picnic. We were on our way back to Knoxville, lounging in the hay with our girlfriends – in the back of a stake-body truck. Six watermelons left from the picnic were rolling around in the hay causing discomfort to all the cuddling couples. We decided to break open the melons, eat the hearts out and chuck the remainder over the side of the truck. The melons broke in many irregular pieces as we banged them together and began to eat. Just as we were getting ready to jettison some of the pieces, we discovered that there was a tomato field literally below us as the truck maneuvered down the "S" curves. About fifteen sun-tanned farm boys were picking tomatoes. What a target! We pounded them good with the watermelon rinds, knocking over their bean baskets full of tomatoes and bouncing rinds off the heads of the boys. We were hysterical. We rolled in the hay, laughing ourselves into ecstasy. My brother, Lynn, shouted, "For God's sake, look up ahead!" The truck was proceeding down the mountain, had made a near U-turn, and we were on the road below the tomato field.

The country boys had lined the field along the road with bean baskets full of tomatoes. We had no place to run. There has never been a tomato bombardment as intense. The boys were running along the field throwing some of the largest Tennessee tomatoes you have ever seen. We received direct hits, and some hit the stake-body and splattered everyone in the truck. When we finally passed the tomato war zone, our casualties were many. The truck was blood-red with tomato juice. We were all covered in red juice and tomato seeds. Lynn said, "If we had a little bread and butter, we could have another picnic right here."

CHAPTER 13

1150 ELEANOR STREET

IT WAS A SMALL FRAME HOUSE on a 50 foot lot (75 feet deep). In 1934, a new era in the life of our family was forged the day Mother and Daddy were able to buy this house. We had longed to have our own house and not live with my Father's parents. Our Mother was especially happy to have this freedom once again. They paid less than $2,000 for the house – with payment, without interest, for about ten years.

After World War II, the house was upgraded with asbestos shingles and was painted yellow. The awning around the screened front porch matched the house. Our Mother insisted on the proper matching colors. The front of the house was shaded by a large maple tree that cooled the front porch on summer afternoons.

There was nothing pretentious about the house. It was our home from the time I was in the second grade until I went into the Navy during World War II.

Soon after we moved to the house, my Father closed in about half of the large back porch as a bedroom for my brother, Lynn and me. The room was too far from the furnace to be heated. Winter was rather cold in our room because we insisted on plenty of fresh air at night. After a very cold night, we could make tracks on the floor as we grabbed our clothes to dress in the warm bathroom. We slept under several heavy quilts and kept very warm in the cold room. We were seldom sick or suffered from colds.

For Lynn and me, our bedroom was "our place". We used it as we wanted as long as we were not too destructive. We knew instinctively not to be destructive and to protect this treasure of "our" house, but we had our accidents.

We used the bed as a wrestling mat when we pretended to be professional wrestlers. Once, when the room was still rather new, we were having a match on the mattress, trying to push the other off the "mat". I hooked my big toe in the rolled edge of the mattress for extra leverage. As I pushed, my foot slipped and punched a large hole in the plasterboard. Our actions were automatic. We began immediate action to repair the damage before Daddy discovered our carelessness. The break was a clean break, about two feet long, but still hinged on one side. We pulled it snuggly together. The joint made an invisible seam to prevent discovery.

Every afternoon after school, we played some sport according to the season. One afternoon, we practiced football drop-kicks over the house. The roof over our bedroom was low and flat and became steeper toward the center of the house. We kicked from the backyard over our bedroom roof, and the ball gradually went over the higher part of the roof. After each of us had had several good kicks over the house, I muffed one that went like a shot through one of the three panes in the top of our bedroom window.

Our Daddy was due home within thirty minutes, so we had to work fast. We took a screwdriver and pried all the broken glass from the window so that it wouldn't appear broken. Meticulously, we picked up every particle of glass fragments from inside and outside the window. We pulled the shade halfway over the window to help camouflage our handiwork.

The broken pane made our room even colder than normal. The wind on a cold night would flap the shade with a snapping noise. The long winter passed without a word about the broken window. In the spring, my brother and I had enough money to buy the glass for the window.

While we were repairing it, our Daddy came into the room and helped us. "It's about time you boys repaired this window. It has been broken almost all winter." He had a little smile on his face. The house was short on closet space. This was an old house, and the closets were very shallow and narrow. My Mother subtly suggested that the end of a hallway as dead space and would make an excellent place for a closet.

My Dad worked with steam engines and was accustomed to knocking steel around, bolting metal together; and, in general, not being very neat. A carpenter he wasn't. He wanted to please my Mother, so he set out on the project one early Saturday morning while Mother was shopping with a friend downtown. Buying new lumber was out of the question. Everything was always built with existing supplies. We had stacked in the basement some 1" x 4" lumber that my Dad had used for concrete forms when he had made a sidewalk around the house. It was rough lumber, not finished with the usual planed surfaces. It was so rough that it looked hairy. He banged on the pieces of wood with his hammer and knocked most of the concrete from the boards.

We stayed clear of the project. He was always asking us to run to the toolbox in the basement and bring him an awl, or a drawknife; and we didn't have the slightest idea what he was talking about. Sometimes when he would be working on a piece of machinery, his favorite request was for 5/8" box and wrench or a wedge or a 7/8" tap with washer. We learned to stay away from projects to keep from hearing a lecture on tools or which was the larger wrench.

Dad worked most all day hammering and sawing and nailing boards in place. He had just finished as my Mother arrived from her trip downtown. We were excited to greet her with the good news that Daddy had made a closet while she was gone.

We made our way through the house to the hall project. Dad stood like a proud kid looking for approval for his daylong project. All of us stopped and looked with amazement at the barn-like construction. There were one-inch gaps between each vertical board. The door was about five feet wide with boards forming an "X" across its face. He had used some huge old hinges from a garage door that must have been eight inches wide coming to a point on each end. He also used the old clasp that held the garage doors closed to secure the closet door.

In that moment of silence, Mother walked up to the door and opened it. She stuck her head well inside the closet and like a Jersey cow, she said, "Moo!"

Dad picked up his tools and took them to the basement and returned to the living room where he quietly read the paper.

CHAPTER 14

MRS. WELLS AND THE DAHLIA BUSH

IN 1936, WHEN I WAS 12 years old, we organized and structured our lives during summer vacations as it suited us. We had ninety days of hot summer to create for ourselves those activities that pleased us most. The emphasis should be on the creativity. There was no adult organization to make our plans – it was ours to do.

When we wanted to buy something, we did not go to our parents and ask for money; we got out the old push mower and cut grass. The one yard we liked to cut most was the yard of Mrs. Wells on Third Avenue. The yard was rather small, and the grass was easy to cut with the push mower. The only drawback were the numerous shrubs, flower beds and dahlia bushes. She loved to raise plants, and she caressed and talked about them as though they were her children. She knew the history of each plant – when and where she obtained it, its record of blooms, and how often she watered and fertilized.

She was very particular about how her yard was cut. She insisted that the sparse grass under the shrubs and plants be trimmed, and no grass clippings should be left on the concrete sidewalks. We always had to sweep the walks, and put the clippings into her paper-lined garbage can.

It was a warm, June morning when Bob Reagan, my brother, Lynn, and I decided to lend our bodies to manual labor for a few cents. Our first thought was to mow Mrs. Wells' yard. It was close to our house. When we arrived at Mrs. Wells' house, with the push mower and sickle, we noticed that the grass was a little higher than usual, so we felt we had a sure job. She agreed to have her yard cut and stood on the front porch, as usual, waving her hands, giving detailed directions as to how to cut the grass and trim under the plants and shrubs. We could have finished the job in fifteen minutes, but Mrs. Wells felt that a good job should take at least an hour.

We mowed carefully around each plant and shrub, making sure not to disturb the precious "children". We finished the mowing, the trimming, swept the walks and disposed of the clippings.

I was knocking on the door to summon Mrs. Wells for her final inspection, when Bob discovered a few stray pieces of grass under her favorite dahlia bush. Quickly, he grabbed the sickle and swished the blade under the bush. All horror struck us! The dahlia tottered a moment and slowly fell like a Georgia pine. This was her favorite plant!!

As we stood frozen for a moment, I could hear Mrs. Wells' footsteps as she was coming to the door.

Immediate creativity came into play. Bob pushed the plant aside, dug his hands a full twelve inches into the earth, where the dahlia previously stood. He then grabbed the stalk of the plant and crammed it into the hole in an up-right position. His hands became machines as he packed the earth tightly around the base of the plant.

We were still numb as Mrs. Wells strolled around the yard as though she were inspecting a plantation. We followed her. Bob tried to stand between her and the dahlia, but she managed to fondle the plant. It stood firm.

At last, she dug down in her apron pocket and produced three nickels, handing each one of us our share. We thanked her for her generosity. One block away was Buffett's Grocery Store. We pushed the mower down the street and leaned it against the storefront. We did not talk much. We strolled into the store like miners on payday – each selecting an ice-cold RC Cola. It was the only cola with a full 12 ounces.

We sat on the curb in the shade, relaxing from the high stress. We never cut Mrs. Wells' yard again.

CHAPTER 15

THE CAT AND PAPER SHOES

ON HOT SUMMER DAYS DURING SCHOOL vacation, we would lie on the front porch in the shade and tell tall tales. Mother kept the porch waxed to a high gloss just like the floors inside the house. The awning shaded the porch, allowing a cool breeze.

Often the unsuspecting cat, stretched out in the cool, would become the source of much fun. We would get a paper sack, and tear pieces large enough to cover the cat's paws and secure the "paper shoes" with a rubber band around the cat's legs. When we had shoes on all four feet, we would allow the cat to touch his feet on the porch.

It would start slowly – a kick with one foot, then another – trying to loosen the paper. But when his feet hit the floor, he would fire-up all cylinders, spinning his feet on the waxed floor. Then, with his ears laid back and his tail straight and stiff, he would shoot across the porch like a rocket. He was a large cat, but he could zip between banisters two-inches apart and leap from the porch.

Around the house, and down the alley, he would go at unbelievable speed.

Two or three days later, the old cat would show-up with rubber bands around each leg and worn- out paper shoes.

Mother would scold us, and take the cat inside-removing the remnants of the fun and feed the cat.

CHAPTER 16

HOME BREW

EVERYONE WE KNEW MADE HOME BREW – or wine. This was the time of Prohibition with no legal alcohol sales possible. Each family learned the technique of making their own spirits. Every household seemed to have a large supply of green bottles. I don't know where they came from, but anytime we were in anyone's basement, the green bottles were there. Another fixture was the ever-present 5-gallon crock and coil of rubber hose. All grocery stores sold malt, along with the yeast and other fixings needed for the brew. I think we developed a nation of brewmasters.

When the brew was "working", it was in the crock with a cloth over the top. The yeast aroma could never be hidden, even if the crock was in the basement. Somewhere in the process, after several weeks, the liquid was strained through a cloth and was then siphoned through the rubber hose into the green bottles. Then came the final act of putting the caps on the bottles. The caps were bought by the box at the store. The capper was a metal rig that had a hand lever. The bottles were placed under a small cup-like part of the capper. When the lever was pressed, the metal caps with a cork insert were crimped on to the bottle top.

Although our Mother, having been raised as a staunch Methodist, was very much against drinking and never touched a drop herself, she helped our Dad in this operation. She usually did the capping and allowed me to help, but we never participated in the mixing, straining and bottling process.

After the filing and capping, the bottles were lined up on the basement shelves with uniform precision. Because the brewing expertise was not very exact, some batches, after a period of time, would begin to explode. All hours of the day and night, we would hear explosions in our basement. Most anyone would know what was happening in the basement. It was proof positive that someone had made a bad run of home brew.

One particular week we were having a revival at our church, and each family was asked to provide a meal for the visiting evangelist and the host pastor. My Mother felt it was a privilege to invite the Cloth to our house to sample her expert cooking. I remember she cooked a roast, vegetables and dessert of pecan pie.

My brother and sister and I had to wait in the living room while the adults ate because there wasn't room enough around the kitchen table. The aroma enticed our hunger far beyond normal limits. We would sneak to the door and peek into the kitchen to determine when we would be able to eat.

Suddenly, there was an explosion in the basement with a thump under the kitchen floor. Then another, and another. There was no home brew in the basement. Mother and Dad, a few weeks before, had bottled tomato juice. Like home brew, a bad run would explode in the bottles.

Our Dad and Mother became more anxious with each explosion and explained that the cause was tomato juice. The minister had a look of "That's a likely story." -- but went along with the explanation.

As the explosions became more numerous and Dad became more guilty, he jumped to his feet and demanded that the ministers accompany him to the basement.

They returned, brushing the juice from their suits, and one of the ministers was wiping his glasses clear. My Dad had a satisfied grin on his face, and my Mother seemed more serene. The ministers looked as though they had marked up another one to experience.

CHAPTER 17

ROLLING TIRES

THE AUTOMOBILE TIRE WAS A REFLECTION of the mood of the time. In the 1930's, the automobile was the magic chariot and offered excitement and adventure to the world. Automobile tires became personified into pets or pals that were valued with high esteem. We rolled them everywhere. Tires were narrower than they are today. The 600 x 16 was a popular size. Some older tires were narrower. When the balloon tires hit the market, they were a prize for rolling. A balloon, white-wall tire, made a person a real sport. Some boys considered the small Austin tire the best roller.

The technique of rolling a tire was simple. The tire was placed on its tread and pushed with a light touch. Guiding was controlled by the direction of the push and also by holding a hand on the outside or inside of the tire. An experienced tire-roller could have the tire roll along beside him, toughing the tire every now and then, at the speed of his walking – like a dog walking beside you.

Tires were our constant companions. When on summer vacation, we would get up early, get our tire that was leaned against the garage the night before, and start rolling toward a friend's house.

When we were short of ideas, we would sit under one of the huge maple trees on Eleanor Street and plot our course of action to more excitement. One of the great contests was to see who had the fastest tire. The hills in Knoxville rivaled those in San Francisco. When we had a tire race, we would choose a long, downhill run of several blocks. Usually, the race was down Wells Avenue, starting at Broadway, and ending at 6th Avenue – a run of seven blocks. The first few Blocks from Broadway, past Gratz, Luttrell, Eleanor, to 3rd Avenue, were downhill. The street leveled off for one block between 3rd and 4th Avenue, past Buffett's Grocery Store, then a sharp downhill again, past 5th Avenue, and Blair's Grocery Store, ending at 6th Avenue. Six or eight boys, some barefoot and others in ragged tennis shoes, would gather on the hill at Broadway with automobile tires of all sizes lined up from curb-to-curb on Wells Avenue and ready for the race. On signal, the race would start with each boy slapping his tire forward as he ran alongside. As the speed of the tires increased, the boys began to lag behind. By the time the tires approached Luttrell Street, they were running free, as their owners were running hard, but were far behind and some distance apart. Most tires became croppers after hitting the curb and being knocked off course. Others hit houses, cars or were entangled in shrubbery.

Once J. C. Lowery had a white-walled balloon tire that navigated the whole course on its own. It crossed Luttrell Street unattended by human hands, then proceeded across Eleanor and 3rd. The tire was steady on its tread as it leaned into the slight curve in front of Buffett's store. It was at this point we lost sight of the tire as it rounded the curve and headed for 4th Avenue. The entire gang of boys was cheering the tire on as we followed in a dead run a block behind. We arrived at 6th Ave., out of breath from the seven block run, just in time to see a man in a checked cap and sport coat put the tire in the rumble seat of his Ford convertible. As he drove off, we noticed that the balloon whitewall matched his tires perfectly. J. C. was upset to have lost his tire, but he had the consolation of knowing that he had the admiration of all of his friends.

1930 Gay Street, Knoxville, TN

Lynn Armstrong and Dan Armstrong – 1931

Ruth Burkhart Armstrong
Wedding Day – 1922

Knoxville, TN, Police Department (early 1900's)
(Left-to-right) – Pat Conley, James Walker, John B. Armstrong

59

1926 Hupmobile

Hupmobile built cars from 1908 to 1941. Robert and Louis Hupp wére founders.

Their cars finally had electric lights installed in 1914. By 1923 they selling 38,000 units per year.

Hupmobile – 1926 (Exterior)

Balloon tires were added in 1925, the year when Hupmobile began an 8-cyclinder engine.

This 1926 Hupmobile has a 6-cyclinder engine, which was the first Hupmobile built a 6. The car cost about $1,295.00.

Hupmobile – 1926 (Interior)

1150 Eleanor St., Knoxville, TN – 1933

Dan, Martha, Lynn Armstrong – Fountain City, TN – 1930

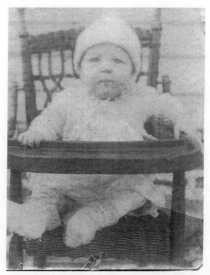

Dan Armstrong – 3 mos. – 1924

Dan Armstrong – 11 mos. – 1924

(Left-to-right) Dan, Darak & Lynn Armstrong, Knoxville, TN – 1929

Darak Armstrong (right), soldier on (left) – (unidentified)
Paris, France, 1917, WWI

First picture on left: 1918 Knoxville, TN – (Left-to-right) Georgia Armstrong, Unidentified, Ruth Burkhart Armstrong, Leta Armstrong Clinton, Ethel Burkhart,

Top right picture: (in car) 1917 Knoxville, TN – Ruth Burkhart Armstrong (at steering wheel), (Left-to-right) Unidentified woman, unidentified man, Leta Armstrong Clinton, Ethel Burkhart

Picture in center of page: 1917 Burkhart Farm, Asbury, TN – (Left-to-right) Ethel Burkhart, Ruth Burkhart Armstrong

Picture in oval: 1904 – (Left-to-right) Ethel Burkhart, Ruth Burkhart Armstrong, Gladys Burkhart, Elmer ("Buck") Burkhart

Picture top left: 1927 – Dan Armstrong, Ruth B. Armstrong

Picture top right: 1926 – Ruth B. Armstrong, Etta Burkhart, Georgia Armstrong, Dan Armstrong, Dog – "Jerry"

Picture bottom left: 1930 – Charles Street Home, Fountain City, TN

Picture bottom right: 1930 – Martha Armstrong, Fountain City, TN

Top picture: 1928 – Lynn Armstrong

Bottom picture: 1926 Atlantic Avenue, Knoxville, TN –
(Left-to-right) B.F. Clinton ("Tinky"), "Jerry", Dan Armstrong

Top left picture: 1929 Inskip, TN – Dan Armstrong

Top right picture: 1929 Inskip, TN – Dan Armstrong,
Lynn Armstrong (on handlebars)

Bottom picture: 1929 Inskip, TN – (Left-to-right) Lynn Armstrong,
Ruth Armstrong, Dan Armstrong

Left picture: 1937 Knoxville, TN – (Left-to-right) Lynn Armstrong, Dan Armstrong, Darak Armstrong, Martha Armstrong

Right picture: 1929 Inskip, TN – (Left-to-right) Ruth Armstrong, Lynn Armstrong, Dan Armstrong

Top picture: 1930 Fountain City, TN – (Left-to-right)
Dan Armstrong, Lynn Armstrong, Martha Armstrong

Bottom picture: 1930 Fountain City, TN – (Left-to-right) Dan Armstrong (in front), Darak Armstrong, Lynn Armstrong, Martha Armstrong, Ruth Armstrong

71

Left picture: 1918 Knoxville, TN – Ruth Burkhart, Darak Armstrong

Right picture: 1930 Fountain City, TN – Darak Armstrong, Ruth Armstrong

Top picture: 1930's Knoxville, TN – Georgia Armstrong

Left picture: 1930's Knoxville, TN – John Armstrong

Right bottom picture: 1930's Joppa, TN – John Armstrong

1930's Knoxville, TN – Smokies Baseball Team

2005 Knoxville High School, Knoxville, TN – Dan Armstrong

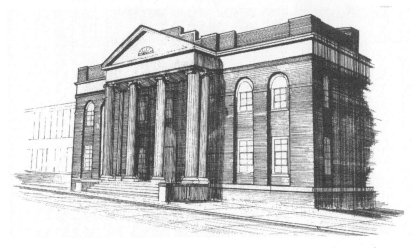

1911-1975 Knoxville, TN – Cumberland Presbyterian Church on Broadway

1984 Lithona, GA – Ruth Armstrong

1969 Knoxville, TN – Darak Armstrong

CHAPTER 18

THE WOODEN GARAGE

THE SMELL OF THE OLD WOODEN garage was magic. The large black circles from years of parked cars losing oil by the drip adorned the floor of every garage.

There was this aroma of burned oil that infiltrated every board in the garage floor. It wasn't a pungent odor – it was a mixture of pinewood and oil that gave a garage its special smell.

There were always dozens of nails in the walls holding all manner of cast-off items. Old tires, inner tubes, washboards, all collected dust for years on the walls. Old phonebooks and years' passed license plates nailed to the wall.

Some innovative person built a loft in back of the garage, a throwback to the hayloft in horse- and-buggy days. This allowed the hood of a car to be driven under the loft nearly up to the windshield; thus, utilizing maximum space for storage.

Garage doors were always the same. They sagged on the rusty hinges and dragged the ground. To open or close, one had to lift the doors slightly to overcome the drag.

Few garages had locks. A large block of wood nailed to one door locked most doors. It was twisted to go across both doors to serve as a lock holding both doors closed. Garages were never finished like a house. There were always cracks between the vertical boards on the exterior. Sometimes garages were painted, and sometimes the raw wood was allowed to weather and age without the benefit of paint.

A garage wasn't part of the house. Garages somehow were not considered as part of the civilized world. It was just a necessary appendage of society to protect the car and store things not needed or wanted in the house.

There was the status issue as well. As TV antennas were indicators of TV ownership in the 1950's, a garage was a prestige item. If you had a garage, you surely must own an automobile. In the 50's, many people owned TV antennas who didn't own TV's – so it was with garages.

Our Grandfather had a garage that was entered from a narrow alley. He always parked his 1929 Hupmobile under cover. To get into the garage, he came down a narrow alley, and made his first partial turn. He would then back into the neighbor's fence, pushing it back to increase the width of the alley. Then, he would swing into the garage. He wasn't a great driver. He just moved things around to make room.

For young boys, the garage was the secret place, the hideout – the place to build things or a place to explore the warehouse of things stored away – a museum of magic things.

We had a garage that had weathered for years without the benefit of paint. My Father, with the zeal to refresh the looks of our garage, was moved to paint the dried boards that had gaps of more than an inch between them. These spaces made wonderful spy holes to peep out of when hiding in the dark garage but did nothing for the beauty of the construction.

After he had painted several boards, he glanced back; and the first board showed no signs of paint. So, with some confusion, he went back and painted the first board. He moved on down the wall; and two other boards appeared to have been missed. After painting them, he moved on, only to discover other boards that seemed to have been missed. The old, dry boards were drinking up the paint. He moved the paint bucket away from the wall for fear that the dry boards would drink the paint from the bucket. Later, when more boards appeared paintless, he threw the bucket of paint on the boards and gave up.

CHAPTER 19

THE WIDOW'S HOUSE

THERE WAS A WIDOW THAT LIVED on 3rd Avenue. She was a gruff old gal that threatened to shoot anyone who cut through her yard to get to the next street.

She was rather rotund, wore long dresses and heavy shoes. In the summer, she always wore a wide-brimmed hat. I don't ever recall seeing her face. She was a woman of mystery, a person to be feared – the type person one talked about in ghost stories.

Sometimes we would gamble and take the short-cut down her unpaved driveway from the street to the alley, then, up the alley for several hundred feet, then an acute right, down another neighbor's driveway to our street. This maneuver saved us from walking about two blocks via the street.

Hugh Morgan lived on 3rd Avenue next door to the widow. There was an empty field between their houses.

One late January afternoon in 1939, Hugh and I were at his house playing with an old Woodstock typewriter, typing all the dirty words we could think of. We were in his bedroom, and his parents were sitting in the living room. We were having a hilariously good time when I realized that it was past time for me to be home.

It was dark when I left his house. I stopped under the streetlight as I pondered the possibilities of taking the short-cut through the widow's yard or going the long way around. The short-cut idea won – I could be home within five minutes that way.

I walked slowly down the driveway, in the darkness. There were no lights on in the house. She, obviously, was in bed. I had nothing to fear. Suddenly, just as I was alongside the porch, the bedroom light flashed on! Visions of jailbreaks and spotlights from a James Cagney movie rambled through my mind as I hit full stride down the driveway toward the darkness of the alley.

I just knew that she must have the shotgun leveled at my backside at that very moment. So, I did a Jesse Owens down the driveway and turned into the pitch-black alley, when, suddenly, in the darkness, something hit me and turned me a complete flip – landing me on my feet. I kept running. I was numb from head-to-foot, as I crashed through a heavy hedge fence, across the Dobsons' backyard, down a driveway, across Eleanor Street and into my house. My Dad said something as I passed the living room door down the hall to my room. I didn't want to allow anyone to see my condition. Time and time again, my Dad had told me not to cut through anybody's property without permission. He was super-protective of private property, especially the property of someone else. He always wanted to be law-abiding. "Never tamper with Government Property or trespass on another person's land." I had visions of living a lifetime in striped suits, working or breaking rocks into gravel, if we violated this code. And, now, I was a criminal for trespassing. But, if I could keep the secret, I might be able to pull off this caper without serving time in a walled prison in some far-off place.

I was amazed that I had no pain. I locked the bedroom door so that my brother, Lynn, and I could examine my wounds. My face was scratched and bleeding from breaking through the hedge. Then, as I removed my coat and shirt, we could find no wounds, no blood. The damage must have been to my butt. We removed my pants and undershorts. No blood! No shotgun pellets! No damage anywhere. This was a miracle!! Divine healing?

The next morning before school, I went down the alley which was bathed in sharp, winter sunshine. After examining the hedge fence, I could see that my route the night before was obvious. The fence was about ten feet high, and the hedge was like a wall of small trees with two strands of barbed wire woven through them. They presented an impossible place to penetrate. But – it wasn't impregnable. There was the opening – a neat passage parting several hedge boughs and two broken strands of rusty, barbed wire.

Further down the alley, near the widow's driveway, the mystery began to unravel. There lay a Christmas tree with its wooden stand in place. It was a perfect vaulting machine. I had turned the corner in the darkness, and the wooden stand on the tree had caught me waist-high and vaulted me a complete flip into the darkness.

As I eased by the widow's driveway and on toward school, I glanced back at the sun-lit alley, remembering how mysterious it was the night before and how non-threatening it was in the light of day.

CHAPTER 20

REVENGE ON THE RAYMONDS' HOUSE

It was a dark, windy night when we gathered in the basement of the Regan house. We put newspapers over the high basement windows. This was a secret meeting, and we knew there must be many other people interested in our secret plans.

The reason for the meeting was motivated by getting revenge on Mr. Raymond who, in his usual manner, had scooped up two tennis balls and one golf ball that had gone into his yard while we were playing in the street. We also felt that he had called the police on several occasions to prevent us from playing in the street in front of his house.

We sat on boxes in a close circle in front of the coal-fired furnace. A candle in the center of the circle caused flickering shadows on the brick basement walls. Bobby, who always liked to keep the tension and excitement running at a fevered pitch, hushed the group with "I think I hear something outside in the driveway." It could be no other than Mr. Raymond sneaking over to listen-in on our secret meeting.

Silence fell over the group as Bob, his hand behind his ear, carried the candle to the papered window. The candle flame set fire to the newspapers! Suddenly, the whole basement seemed to be ablaze and full of smoke. We frantically began beating out the fire with our coats. Bob's Father, a Methodist minister, opened the basement door and shouted down the stairs, "Bob! Are you burning something down there?" Bob explained that he had just opened the furnace door to throw in some paper. That seemed to quiet that issue.

The meeting again settled down to serious plotting. Sam suggested that he burn Mr. Raymond's house. We did not take this seriously, and this was overruled with the suggestion that we throw paint on his front porch from some of the old paint cans in the basement. Suggestion after suggestion flowed from the group until we arrived at the *coup d'etat.*

We knew that the Raymonds were spooky people, afraid of their own shadows. So – "Let's scare them. Let's use the old squeaking-screen trick." But, this would require one brave soul, sneaking in the dark over the hedge and across a no-man's section of yard and attaching a pin to the screen of the Raymond's house. He would need to be very careful that the black thread attached to the pin did not get fouled in the hedge. Mr. Raymond had threatened to shoot anyone be caught in his yard. Sam said, "Give me the pin." He was always a reckless kid. We stood as one and patted him on his back for his daring. We knew that Mr. Raymond sat in his living room in the dark watching everything that was going on in the neighborhood. We went across the street from his house with the candle and burned a newspaper in a sewer to attract his attention while Sam slithered across the open yard and attached the pin.

We gathered again in the darkness of the basement hideout. The thread was drawn tight from the screen through the basement window. We squeezed the thread with the damp cloth between the thumb and forefinger and rubbed the thread. A squeaking sound was magnified in the window screen like a screech owl. The Raymonds' front porch light came on, and Mr. Raymond peered out from behind the door, looking both ways, but never venturing out on the porch.

We were doubled-up with laughter on the dark basement floor. We had to keep it subdued to prevent Mr. Raymond from hearing. Here was the feared evil force showing his true fearful nature.

When the porch light went off, we continued our relentless squeaking screen attack until a police car whipped around the corner, and two husky policemen came up on Mr. Raymond's porch. We were scared to death. What if they found the pin and followed the threat back to our basement hideout? We will spend the remainder of our lives in jail. The policemen seemed so close. Even though we were in the darkness, we felt very exposed.

"Pull the string! Pull the string!", the excited group shouted together in hushed tones. We yanked the thread. It is surprising how strong a thread can be. It seemed to stretch instead of breaking. After another quick jerk, the tension was released, and we reeled the thread in. To our surprise, the pin had dropped out of the screen. What a relief! No evidence left behind. Every bit of thread and the pin were in our hands. "Throw it in the furnace", we chimed, as one fearful voice. The evidence was destroyed.

As the police searched the yard around the Raymonds' house, each of us made our way to our homes with a smile on our faces.

CHAPTER 21

PUSHCARTS

IN 1933, WHEN JOBS WERE VERY scarce, men and sometimes entire families, would gather paper and cardboard and sell it to a dealer who recycled it into reusable paper.

This was a big business in Knoxville, Tennessee. The streets would be full of homemade carts carrying paper to the dealer. The carts would be built up on the side with sheets of cardboard to a height of ten to twelve feet, so as to increase the hauling capacity. To get a cart full meant pushing the cart many miles through alleys. A whole load, sometimes representing a day's work, would bring one dollar.

It was a very hot July day as I hurried up Kenyon Avenue toward my friend's house. I hopped from the hot sidewalk to the grassy strip next to the street to keep my bare feet cool. The houses in this neighborhood were very large and well-kept.

As I hopped from grass to sidewalk and back again, I noticed a large, partially-filled cart parked at the curb in the shade of a silver maple tree. A tall, black man, about sixty-years old, had just removed a cake tin from a box on the back of his cart. He sat in the shade on a granite wall that held the yards in check on Kenyon Avenue. He had begun to pry the lid off the cake tin, but stopped as I approached. He looked like a kind man in laundered and pressed bib overalls. He wore a ragged straw hat.

I sat down beside him. His first words were, "The Lawd sure made a fine day for us." His voice was gentle, and he spoke to me like a father to his sons. He fanned himself with his old straw hat as he held tightly to the cake tin in his lap. I asked him about his cart. He had made it from wood scraps, and he had found the two wheels in a junk pile. After a quick rest, I was up and on my way. I looked back to say "good-bye" but was horrified at what I saw. He tried to shield my eyes with the cake tin lid, so I could not see the contents.

But – I saw. He had garbage for his lunch – a half-eaten corn-on-the cob, scraps of bread, other pieces of half-eaten food that he had salvaged from garbage cans.

I looked away to keep from embarrassing him. I felt sick.

My feet moved faster and faster, as my heart felt deep sorrow. I ran, but did not feel the hot sidewalk.

I ran away from the horror as did the world. It was another thirty years before men of color and dignity could stand their full height and not eat garbage.

CHAPTER 22

KNOXVILLE SMOKIES

THE SMITHSON STADIUM, ALSO KNOWN AS Caswell Park, was the professional baseball park of my youth. It was the home of the Knoxville Smokies who usually occupied the Southern League cellar. The Atlanta Crackers were usually the team to beat. The Birmingham Barons, Memphis Chicks, Little Rock Travelers, Chattanooga Lookouts, Asheville Tourists were also members of this popular league.

It was said that Knoxville could batter the boards in the fence with their hitting but couldn't catch a groundball in a net.

The St. Louis Cardinals came to town for an early spring exhibition game. The kids packed the stadium to see Dizzy Dean and his brother Paul Daffey. Paul pitched most of the game, and Diz just trotted around the field late in the game to the cheers of a lot of happy kids.

We had a pitcher by the name of Leo Moon. He was a Southpaw and a pretty good pitcher for a country boy playing in the Minor Leagues. Leo came in late in the game. St. Louis was ahead by two runs and had the look of wanting to get on the train for Budtown. We were proud that Leo pitched so well – not allowing a St. Louis hit in the 8th and first-half of the 9th. Local pride began to swell in the hearts of all the kids. Two Smokies made it on base in the bottom of the 9th as the shadows in the ballpark began to cover the infield. Everyone was tense because we might have a chance to beat a big league team. Who should come to the plate but Leo Moon. Everyone moaned, and there was murmur of "double-play". Everyone knew that pitchers were not good hitters, especially against a Dean. Paul Dean rubbed up the ball as he looked knowingly around the infield. The crowd became restless, and some began to pick up their cushions, ready to depart.

Paul dipped his body forward and fired a blazer across the middle of the plate. Moon didn't move, as the crowd shuffled and fell silent. They could see the "handwriting on the wall". Paul tugged at his pants, and picked up some dirt from the mound. His next pitch came in fast and low, and Leo swung a dipping swing and hit the ball on the end of the bat. The ball started low, gradually became higher and higher, and higher over the Pabst Blue Ribbon sign in right center field. The crowd roared, and threw cushions and programs in the air as Leo jumped and danced around the bases, while the St. Louis boys rapidly left the field.

Leo was the only man on the field when he came home to a standing ovation from every kid in Knoxville. Leo Moon became a household word that night. I understand Moon enjoyed his celebrity status and Tennessee White Lightning for several days.

When I arrived home, I rehashed every detail of the game. I knew exactly how Leo hit that low pitch over the board fence. I remembered it then, and I remember it now. It still thrills me.

I guess I will always be excited when the underdog in a seemingly hopeless situation becomes the conqueror over impossible odds. To the Cardinals, it was just another Exhibition Game. For us, Leo Moon was the symbol of hope for all of us. He was our hero.

CHAPTER 23

KNOT-HOLE GANG

THE KNOT-HOLE GANG WAS AN UNOFFICIAL card-carrying group of kids that gathered outside the outfield fence of Caswell Park in Knoxville on game day to watch the game through a knot-hole in the pine-board fence. Of course, most of the knot-holes were cut in the fence with a pocket knife. Early in the morning, while on my way to Park Junior High School, Hugh Morgan and I would ride our bicycles behind the fence and cut a knot-hole only to discover on game day that some adult had commandeered the hole. Several hundred kids and adults would claim a spot on the fence. The police would patrol the area causing everyone to step back from the fence when they appeared and then immediately hurried back to their positions once the patrol moved on. The pine boards were slick around the holes caused by sweat, tears, and oil from human skin. The fence became a mass of "knot-holes" through the years, causing the management to install a metal fence outside the old wooden one. There was about a foot between the two fences that could be discovered if a person climbed on top of the fences.

A stroke of brilliance struck me – Why not come to the ballpark early and get between the fences and watch the game through one of the old knotholes. No one would ever guess that I was inside the fences. I couldn't be seen.

There was a special enthusiasm about those who couldn't afford a ticket and wanted to see a baseball game so badly that they would stand for nine innings with their eyes pressed against a hole in a pine board fence, cheering the home team. There was an instant loyalty to the local team. We knew all the players by name, their batting averages, and the latest news as to their chances of making it into the Major Leagues.

One of the responsibilities of those who had a knot-hole for the game was to keep the others, who could only hear the cheers of the crowd, informed as to what was happening on the field. We became excellent play-by-play commentators. If a home run was hit toward our area of the fence, we were obligated to those waiting to shout, "Home run! Home run!" And point to the general direction it was going. The waiting crowd would scatter attempting to retrieve an official baseball.

It was a hot July day, and I arrived two hours early. I climbed a chain link fence to the corner of the heavy metal fence and boosted myself on top of the double fence. I crawled to a good spot in left center field and slid between the fences. It was hot in the narrow tomb. The metal fence was a griddle as it fried my back. I adjusted my body to rest on a cross member and stand on a 2' x 4'. It was very uncomfortable, but I was zeroed in on a large knothole. I had a panoramic view of the entire field. "This is a good safe place – no intermittent peeking and looking for the police," I thought to myself. "This is like a grandstand seat for free."

The stands began to hum as a shirt-sleeved crowd began to fill the stands. The "pop" of a ball could be heard hitting the mitt as the pitcher warmed-up by throwing their best stuff to the catcher with his cap on backwards. My blood began to stir with excitement when they rolled out the batting cage, and balls were hit to the outfield.

An outfielder was near the fence. This was the closest I have ever been to a real ballplayer. As he stood waiting for balls to be hit, he adjusted his pants several times. He would chatter-talk to the batter in the cage. "Come on. Hit that pill to the best outfielder in the league.

I can catch anything you can hit." I guess this was pure "psyching-up" because he dropped the first line drive that was hit to him.

The stands were packed and noisy as the rolled the batting cage off the field, and the grounds crew dragged the infield until it was smooth. The umpires came on the field, lead by Steamboat Johnson to a chorus of "boos" from the fans.

I was ready for the game to begin.

The fence suddenly exploded with a rattling noise that seemed to bounce around inside the restricted area between the fences. The police were on the outside of the metal corrugated fence, beating on it with nightsticks. It was like being inside a drum. The terror and the silence that followed caused my hearing to be especially acute. I heard one policeman say to the other, "Charlie, is it yours or my time to shoot through the fence?" "John, I believe it is my time. I am going to use a heavy load in my 38 to be sure to go through both fences." Out from between the fences, I came, slick as an eel, down inside the park onto the outfield grass. Running full speed, I ran behind the center fielder, headed for right field, as the ump yelled, "Time out! Get that kid off the field.!"

I could hear the roar from the crowd, cheering me on. "Run! Run! Run! The right fielder had turned around, looking at me with a friendly, understanding grin. I knew that he had come over the fence when he was younger.

When I made it to the right field foul line in front of the bleachers, a tall policeman was standing like a fortress in front of me. He suddenly turned to look behind the stands. He looked away from me but spoke out of the corner of his mouth, "Get a seat in the bleachers and don't move around, and I won't know where you are."

What a wonderful game. What a wonderful day.

CHAPTER 24

FOUL BALL

HAVING AN ENTIRE OUTFIT IN WHICH to play ball was an impossible dream. Those who had a glove were unusual. Some had a bat. Shoes and uniforms were out of the question. Usually when two sandlot teams played, at least half of the players did not have gloves. Those who possessed a glove usually had a hand-me-down from their father or older brother. When the teams arrived at the field, those without gloves began their desperate search for a player on the other team who would loan a glove.

A serious ritual took place to determine which team would be in the field first and who would be "in town" (who would be at bat firsts). One player from each team would face each other. One would toss a bat, small-end up, so the other could catch it. The catcher always had certain place he wanted to grab the bat, so the tosser attempted to toss it so as to confuse his selection. After the bat was caught in the air, the two players proceeded hand-over-hand toward the small-end of the bat. The object was to grab the last hand hold on the bat, allowing no more space to remain. As their hands approached the end of the bat, it would become obvious who would arrive at the last hand-hole.

Then a shrewd tactical action was called for – "crow-picks!" Instead of using the full fist around the bat, now each player used only his first two fingers in a "V". Up the bat they would go until only a scant bit of the bat would protrude. The last person would catch the bat with his fingernails. A sharp opponent would shout, "Three Hard Kicks!" This meant that his opponent would have to hold on to the bat while the other kicked the bat with the sole of his shoe three times. If the bat were dropped, the kicker could choose either bat or field. But, if he held on, he tossed the bat in the air and was required to catch it below the trademark. If this were successful, he could choose bat or field.

While this process took place, both teams gathered around cheering on the player from their side.

To play ball, having a baseball is essential. We had no money to buy a ball, and anyone who happened to have an old baseball, the ball usually had an "ear" on it where the cover was partly off; or the ball would be covered with black electrician's tape.

Getting a baseball was essential. We worked out a system for getting foul balls that came over the grandstand at Smithson's Stadium. This wasn't easy. They had a foul ball chaser who had an uncanny ability to know where a foul ball was going the instant he ran from inside the grandstand. Behind the grandstand was a large parking lot. Often, the foul ball would rattle around among the cars and would change direction erratically. If a person retrieved a ball among the cars, the ball chaser would seem to be right there. He would take the ball and escort our group member into the ballpark to see the remainder of the game. The ball would be exchanged for admission. We were interested in getting a ball to keep.

We placed about half of our team among the cars. Two were stationed just outside the parked cars in a clear area. About another fifty yards further, we had two of our fastest men. This deployment was used for two ball games before one of our men among the cars retrieved a foul ball. Just as the tough ball chaser closed in, our man stood up and threw the ball into a clearing where it was caught by a short red-headed team mate. He whirled and made a perfect throw to one of our fast men who made a "professional" catch on the run and disappeared in the distance across the Southern Railroad tracks and into the residential section. The ball chaser stood with his arms limp at his side as he stared into the distance. We melted into the scenery.

On one occasion, after being threatened by the ball chaser that he would have us arrested for theft of baseballs if we did it again, we were all in position behind the grandstand – a little apprehensive. We had a big game coming up, and we needed a good baseball. The ball chaser bounded out of the gate on the first foul ball. It rolled under several cars and into the waiting hands of one of our men. The process began with one toss, then another, to one of our fast men, who ran full speed toward the railroad tracks, only to be blocked by a fast-moving freight train. He ran alongside the train, hoping it would pass so that he could cut across the tracks toward our neighborhood. When the train finally passed, he was in a rather tough neighborhood, all by himself. He headed back toward our area, when three toughs with a large German Shepherd on a chain approached. "Look here what the little boy has." They plucked the ball from his hand. "This is an official baseball like the professionals have. It looks like we got us a ball. Now, git out of our area, or we will sic Bruno on you!"

After this, we knew to run in the opposite direction when we retrieved a baseball.

CHAPTER 25

A KIND MAN ON 4ᵗʰ AVENUE

I REMEMBER A MAN WHO LIVED in the 1100 block of 4ᵗʰ Avenue. He and his wife lived in a duplex at the top of the hill. He was a very pleasant man with black curly hair. He was on my paper route – THE KNOXVILLE NEWS SENTINEL (a Scripps-Howard paper). This was in the latter days of the Depression in 1939. The paper was twenty cents per week. I made about seven cents per customer, per week, when everyone paid. I usually cleared about four dollars per week for a seven-day delivery of seventy-five papers.

It always amazed me at the number of people who would not pay the paper boy. Some people would get behind three or four weeks, and then pay one week or even ten cents on their bill. I would keep delivering the paper hoping they would pay. Many never paid.

This is why this man on 4th Avenue was such an outstanding person. He did not have a lot of money. He worked downtown and walked to and from work.

Every Friday night when I collected for the paper, he always gave me twenty-five or thirty-cents. He would always smile his wide Italian smile and say, "Here, buy yourself a coke." Even more, I remember his honest and kind face. He made me feel important and that I meant something to him, and that I was okay. For a kid who had rather low self-esteem, I enjoyed being liked by him.

I do not remember his name. Isn't that the way? We go through life, and there are so many people who make a big difference in our life, and we forget to tell them.

Sometimes when I give a little extra to someone I will say, "Here, buy yourself a Coke." And I see the wide Italian smile in my mind.

CHAPTER 26

THE SALES PITCH

THE SUN HAD BEGUN TO SHINE a little brighter on the economic situation in the world, but money was still very tight at our house.

A lot of companies, sensing the sales' opportunities, were sending commission salesmen, door-to- door, selling brushes, cookware, books and Bibles.

We felt it was absurd for anyone to come to our house because we were not buying – not because we would not want the product, but because we just did not have the money.

Most of the time, the salesmen would be warded-off at the door, but on one occasion, an encyclopedia salesman was extra-pushy and insisted that the family was bound for the pits of ignorance if we did not hear his presentation. He assured my Dad there was no obligation to buy. He just had to give so many presentations each day.

With a flair, my Father bid him come into our living room. It was an exciting time for my brother, my sister and me. It was the first time a salesman had ever made it past the front door.

There was a certain humor about it. All of the family knew that we had no money to buy 50 or 100 books, so it was a joke for him to consider us a prospect.

The young, well-dressed salesman showed us one large volume, leafing through, to show us the numerous illustrations. He stopped at a two-page spread of the anatomy of the human body. "Here you can see clearly the major parts of the human body." My Dad, thinking the whole operation rather humorous, replied, "Yes, I have always been interested in that."

The young salesman was very solemn and took our Dad's comment seriously. He pressed on. All of us hovered around the books, as he "amazed" us with their remarkable contents. We were living in two separate worlds, and we were the only ones aware of it.

The young man's sale's energy approached the crescendo as he displayed before us – right on the very thin place in the rug – his *piece de resistance.* He unfolded a long piece of covered cardboard on which was painted the books as if they would appear if in a bookcase. The display zig-zagged across our carpet. The salesman said, "Well, what do you think?" My Dad, with a slight grin, replied, "They are kinda thin, aren't they?"

We kids fell to the floor in hysterical laughter. The salesman picked up all of his book displays and left the house.

I am sure that he spread the word that we were the most ignorant family in our neighborhood.

We were not ignorant – just broke.

CHAPTER 27

LOVE NOTES

FRANCIS GILMORE WAS MY SWEETHEART WHEN we went to Park Junior High School. The time we were sweet on each other was a difficult time – the boys and girls were divided into separate educational classes as an experiment.

Boys' classes and girls' classes left little, if any, time to fraternize between each session. This separation generated a new enthusiasm for writing love letters during class that could be slipped to our sweetheart as you passed in the hall between classes.

This was a very secret operation for many reasons. The message was secret – the words that were written were out of character for boy talk; no guy wanted the other guys to see his tender side. The letter had to be written in secret in class to prevent the teacher from discovering that verse was taking precedence over algebra. It was against the rules of this new experiment for students to communicate such trivia as "love" in the confines of the educational institution, so all messages had to be transferred with great finesse and secrecy.

Drop points were developed – the potted plant in the hall; the top of the fire extinguisher outside Mrs. Calloway's room; inside the front cover of a certain book in the library; and, of course, the "handshake" in the hallway.

The notes were not some casual expression. They contained the first deep exploration of feeling for another person outside the family. They were attempts of honest expression of feeling that, up to that point in our lives, lay dormant in the dark recesses of our souls.

They were thoughts and feelings that were written to a special person that we had learned to trust. For someone else to read these private expressions between two people was an abrupt invasion that was an emotional tragedy.

One Friday morning, as I came into Mrs. McCampbell's homeroom class, a note to Francis that I had composed the night before slipped from my notebook onto the floor in front of the teacher's desk. Before I could scoop it up and return it to its hiding place, Mrs. McCampbell said, "Let me see that paper." The give-away was the hearts I had drawn on the outside of the paper.

I stood beside her desk in front of the class as she read the note silently. Then she said, "Do you plan to marry this girl?" "Marry! – Marry? I am just a thirteen year-old kid, I thought. For a few minutes, I stood there amazed at the question. Not having a logical answer, I stuttered, "W-w- w-well, no." The class was full of giggles and side remarks.

Mrs. McCampbell looked at me sternly, as only an experienced "old-maid" schoolteacher could – a look developed after many years. "All this 'love' talk should not be said to anyone that you don't plan to marry. I am sending you to the Principal's office to see if he can straighten you out."

When the Principal read the note, he said, "We have been trying to put a stop to his note-writing. Why do you think we have separated the male and female elements of this school?" I shrugged my shoulders. He took this to be insolent behavior. "Mr. Jones is on his way to discipline one of his students. He will show you what it means to be disobedient."

Mr. Jones was noted for a tough attitude toward students. It may have been because he was slight in stature and walked with a swagger as if he were carrying a 45 caliber automatic on each hip. He was quite proud of the hand-crafted paddle he had hanging on the wall in his classroom. He was constantly threatening, daring students to get out of line, so he could use his paddle.

It was a formidable weapon, a highly-lacquered, one-inch thick piece of hardwood, four inches wide, about the length of a baseball bat. He had crafted a handle large enough for both hands. Every few inches of the length was adorned with small holes to raise blisters on the fanny of any recipient.

Mr. Jones burst into the office with Donald Cheek by the arm. Donald was white as a sheet. When I saw that Mr. Jones was carrying his lacquered paddle,. I understood Donald's fear. He was to be the first to face the terror of the big stick. I felt sorry for Donald. He was not well. He had just survived a ruptured appendix and was just now recovering from the near-death experience. The Principal turned and said, "" think that Romeo here needs a taste of that paddle, too." It was like a sentence to the guillotine.

"Which one wants to be first?", said Jones, as he swaggered to the center of the office and cinched up the crotch of his baggy pants. "I will," fell from my numb lips. I grabbed my ankles as he shuffled his feet to get a good position for leverage. The paddle whistled, with all those holes, as he teed-off on me and landed a solid blow on the left cheek of my rear, lifting me off the floor and pitching me against the wall. I was numb. I felt no pain. Jones yelled, "Goddamn". His paddle had broken, leaving only a handle, with a one-inch stick extending the length.

It seemed to be divine intervention to keep Donald from suffering the total power of the intact paddle. In anger, Jones whacked Donald across the rear and on his legs with the stick, stinging him painfully, but not doing serious damage.

Donald and I were heroes. We had taken the worst that they could dish out, and we had broken the symbol of fear. I was sore for a week but swore to the peer group that Jones' best effort had not hurt a bit.

The note writing between Francis and me continued through the school year and persisted during the summer. It was as though it was us against the world. I guess we were beginning to break the absolute bond between ourselves and family and reach to another.

I was a notorious bad speller and always wrote better when I could check with the dictionary. The summer vacation gave me the opportunity to compose longer and more elaborate renditions as compared to those short notes written in haste during school.

One especially amorous letter was composed over a period of two days. Francis was out of town with her family. So, I carried the note in my pocket for fear that someone would find it. Bob Reagan, my brother, Lynn, and I were walking to a movie theater downtown. I checked to be sure I still had my dime in my pocket. The note flipped out and on the sidewalk. All of us made a lunge for it. I managed to roll on the sidewalk and grasp the note. Lynn and Bob pounced on me, attempting to get the love letter from my hand. They were about to overpower me. I knew that for them to have this in their possession would result in my being teased and humiliated. With my last bit of strength, I stretched and dropped the missile into a sewer. It was a great loss for me, but I felt very comfortable that they did not have my written emotions within their grasp. We went to the movie, and I forgot the whole incident, feeling safe that the note was in a ten- foot-deep sewer.

The next afternoon I was sitting on our front steps in the shade of a large tree when I saw Lynn and Bob coming down the street with smiles on their faces. A chill went up my spine. Bob was carrying a twelve-foot cane pole with a nail protruding from the end. The first words they uttered as they approached were, "Dear Frances, I love you."

I lived a hard emotional summer. Francis never understood. She thought I had revealed our secret. Love was never quite the same.

CHAPTER 28

MUD-DOB FIGHTS

FROM TIME TO TIME, THERE SEEMED to be a compulsion within us to build a fort – to live the life of the Knights of old; to defend life and limb in battle.

Back of the Lancaster house on Wells Avenue was a large depression in the land. High on the rim provided an excellent place for the construction of a fort.

Our urge was satisfied by constructing a fort on the rim of the depression facing the alley where boys often came to challenge us. The fort on the rim protected our rear with a sheer drop of about twenty-five feet.

The inside of the fort was dug out about two-feet deep with the red clay piled up on the border around the hole. Large rocks were stacked on the red clay mounds to form a wall with red clay mortar.

We would become scavengers to find briars and other sticky plants to cover the outside front of the fort, about three or four feet deep. This prevented any group overrunning the fort with a frontal attack.

All of us developed a rather good throwing arm, hurling red-clay mud balls at attackers approaching the fort. We would use a broomstick about two or three feet long to ward off attackers before they came close enough to make their mud-dobs effective. A mud-dob was stuck on the end of the stick. The stick was used as though it was an extension of our arm. With a throwing motion, the mud-dob would fly some thirty to forty yards and some times further.

I recall one hectic battle when Bill and Marshall Latham brought some boys from their neighborhood and attacked our fort. The battle lasted for most of one Saturday afternoon until we either ran out of energy or mud.

We left our fort and headed home for supper, when to our dismay, we discovered a horrible sight. Mr. Lancaster, about three weeks previously, had had his large two-story house painted – white. We gazed in amazement, and fear, as we observed that the one side was entirely covered with mud-dobs, sticking to the side of the house. Our long-range shots were longer than we had estimated. Another strange aspect was that no windows were broken. Mud was sticking all around several windows and all over the open spaces, but there were no broken windows.

Mr. and Mrs. Lancaster never mentioned a word to us about the "war" damage. They surely must have been saints to understand the recklessness of boys, or maybe they could recall the fun and excitement of their youth.

CHAPTER 29

THE MAGIC EYE

WHEN I WAS IN HIGH SCHOOL, Lane's Drugstore on Gay Street installed a new innovation to open their front door *The Magic Eye.* The name alone conjured up an air of mystery that brought the high school crowd downtown after school to see this new advancement in science and have a large Coke or cherry smash.

There were two front doors. You might guess that this was no small-town operation. In front of each door, inside and out, were two posts with weird cyclops eyes. An unseen beam of light stretched from one cyclops eye to the other eye across the entrance and exit.

When a person approached the door and broke the beam – Ah hah!! The door swung open before the outreached hand touched the glass. The crowd would line up to go through the door and once inside, would immediately go through the Magic Eye exit side.

Nothing was more fun than introducing an uninformed friend to this modern marvel. We had a cousin that came in from the farm in East Tennessee. In the process of showing him the sites of the downtown, we headed for Lane's Drugstore.

My brother, who was never slow when a possible money-making deal appeared, stood in front of the drugstore and bet our cousin a nickel that he could open the front door without touching any part of the door. Our cousin thought a few minutes and said that he was willing to wager twenty- five cents on the deal. The reason he raised the bet so easily was that he had just sold his prize hog, and he was flushed with greenbacks.

Lynn, my brother, jumped at the idea of making a quick quarter. Of course, he did not have the nickel, much less the quarter. But why does a person need money when he is betting on a sure thing.

Well, Lynn put his hands behind his back and jutted out his chin in pure defiance as he approached the heavy glass door. He walked through the Magic Eye; and with a ""hump" ran chin-first into the door, knocking himself backwards several feet. Blinking with astonishment, he read the small note on the door: "Magic Eye temporarily out of order".

We tried to explain to our cousin about the mysterious way the door opened by itself when it was working, but all he was interested in was his twenty-five cents because he had just outsmarted his city-slicker cousin.

CHAPTER 30

KNOXVILLE HIGHSCHOOL

OUR HIGH SCHOOL WAS VERY LARGE, three stories covering a city block. At the front were huge marble columns and very wide marble steps with a statue of a WWI soldier in full battle dress on the front lawn.

It set the mood for the school in 1941 when the world was at war. We knew that, soon, each of us would be involved. We were proud of our honor ROTC Batallion composed of four companies and a military band. About five hundred students were in uniform.

In my Senior Year, I was Second Lieutenant in charge of the First Platoon of "B" Company. Second Lieutenant Hugh Morgan commanded the Second Platoon. Second Lieutenant, Russell "Rut" Brisco was the happiest kid I ever knew. He could see humor in everything and could bring laughter to the most serious setting. He was in command of the Third Platoon.

The whole ROTC Batallion was gathered in military precision on the front steps of the high school for our annual military photograph. Spit and polished, uniforms in perfect order, caps tilted just right. The photographer's head was under the black cloth. He was on a high stepladder with flash powder gun ready. Everyone in place and posed, except Rut, who came rushing into the scene and hurriedly took his place at the end of a row.

Col. Moore yelled as only a colonel can yell, "Brisco! Where the Hell is your cap?" Rut whipped it out of his belt where he had it tucked. The whole Batallion began to snicker and move in place. We soon settled down to a more military demeanor. Everything was ready and quiet. The photographer stopped. He pointed to Brisco. He was carrying his bag lunch in his left hand. Col. Moore yelled once more, "Brisco!" By this time, the whole unit was in a laughing frenzy.

About thirty minutes later, we finally got the picture. Rut was a joyful person. He could see humor in the dullest of situations. He entered the Air Force upon graduation. He was a P-38 pilot. He was killed in a crash at the War's end.

In chemistry class, four students shared a large table with a lead-lined sink sunk in the center with two curved water faucets.

This class was in constant chaos.

"Iron-Head" Robinson threw sulfuric acid over the class when his hydrogen generator blew up while he was adding more acid. In one class, our chemistry professor was dressed in a new gray, double-breasted suit. Jimmy Bean was laying across his table on his back attempting to stop the faucet from dripping by pushing his thumb over the opening. The pressure built up until Jimmy could not hold the pressure back with both hands. There was a burst of water that covered the prof's new suit in small wet spots, causing him to look like a spotted owl. We had one project in which a lot of bending of glass tubing was involved. This included heating the glass Pyrex tubing before it could be bent into the desired shape. Jimmy Bean broke the end of the tube he was heating. When removed from the heat, the tube returned to its natural color but was still blazing hot. As Jimmy held the tube in tongs, he informed the prof that he had chipped the end of the tube. The professor was lecturing to the class but held out his hand. Jimmy shrugged his shoulders and dropped the hot tube in his hand. For a few seconds, smoke rose from the prof's hand as from a branding iron. "God Damn!" he yelled, throwing the hot tube to the floor. We noticed his hand was bandaged for several days.

We discovered that iron filings mixed with sulfur and heated into a clinker was the base for a stinkbomb when diluted sulfuric acid was poured over the clinker. Outside the Chemistry Lab, there was a huge air intake for the furnace. Need I say how we stunk up the whole school. Several classes had to escape to the outdoors.

The ROTC had a rifle range in the huge attic of the school. Each of us had to qualify on the range. On one occasion, our Company was firing for score. One kid pulled his target back, and he had shots all over the target. M.L. "Baldy" Ault was on the mat next to him. "Baldy" had one problem. He could not sight with his right eye, so he leaned over the rifle and sighted with his left eye. He missed his target completely and hit the one next to his. I believe "Baldy" went into the Army Field Artillery when he graduated.

CHAPTER 31

CHRISTMAS AT THE CHURCH

THE CHRISTMAS TREE AT THE FIRST Cumberland Presbyterian Church on Broadway always touched the ceiling. It filled the church with a pleasant evergreen aroma that enhanced the beauty of the familiar decorations, worn from years of use. Children would circle the huge tree looking for special ornaments. The old friends were remembered from Christmases past.

A few days before the holiday, the entire church gathered for a Christmas party. It was a rather simple, unpretentious gathering, but full of joy. The Sunday School classes exchanged gifts. Awards were given for special activities; and, of course, the fattest man in the church was Santa Claus. The costume was older than some of the men who played the part. I remember one child shouting, "Santa, your face is cracked."

The base of the tree was surrounded by filled brown grocery-store bags. The MacDonald family owned the chain of White Stores in Knoxville. They were members of the church and contributed heavily to its financial strength. Each year they supplied enough candy, nuts, oranges and apples to fill a paper bag for every member of the church.

After the group had sung all the Christmas hymns and popular carols, Santa Claus would move to the paper bags and begin handing them out to the many out-reached hands. This was the most exciting thrill of the night. It was more than just a treat. There seemed to be a closeness like sitting down with the family in a warm and secure home to enjoy a turkey feast.

Some took their sacks home while others sat in little groups exploring all the goodies and sampling the variety of good-tasting treats. There was an abundance of good things. Peace seemed to prevail in the glow of Christmas lights and contented hearts.

For a moment, we felt secure inside this warm circle of friends, while the world outside was cold and raw with the sharp edges of economic hopelessness cutting into everyone's life.

CHAPTER 32

POLITICS

My family always have been Democrats. That affiliation was more deeply ingrained when the Republican Herbert Hoover as elected President in 1928. His election was followed by the economic collapse in 1929.

Hoover was elected because his opponent, Al Smith. suffered from the religious propaganda of the time espoused against Catholics.

I remember well my Presbyterian father sitting at the table in the dimly-lit kitchen, parroting the propaganda, stating that the election of a Catholic would mean that the Pope in Rome would rule the country.

The election of 1928 was a "landmark" period that cast our family's political direction forever into the Democratic party.

In 1928, my father voted for Hoover, his first vote cast for a Republican. For many years afterward, he would often repeat, "I voted for a Republican for President *once*, and I was out of work for nearly two years. NEVER AGAIN!"

This may have been an unfair placing of blame for the economic conditions that were worldwide, but it was a condition that motivated the working-class people to vote for Franklin Roosevelt for President for three terms.

The Depression years weakened but did not extinguish the flame of hope in the American people. Through the Blue Mist, there was always hope. We always stood on the "tiptoes of expectation" looking for a better, brighter time.

We felt that the "Happy Days Were Here Again" when Roosevelt was elected in 1932 and brought about sweeping economic changes.

The railroad was operating again, and our Dad was working four days a week. I remember sometime later when he came home with a broad smile on his face and announced that his salary had been raised to seventy-five cents per hour as a machinist for Southern Railway.

Many of the much-maligned government rescue job programs, as well as conservation programs like the TVA, made a difference. People were working, and they had money in their pockets that helped to lift up their spirit and personal worth. They could provide for themselves.

TVA not only saved East Tennessee and other areas from the annual destructive floods, but provided super phosphate to "green" the red clay land and prevent erosion. The cheap electricity allowed families to replace the old icebox with the electric refrigerator and also to replace the smelly, oil stove with an electric stove.

There was a feeling of progress toward better times, and hope was alive. Occasionally, there were those people who would be upset over the speed of the progress. Some politicians would whine about government control of business saying that the private sector should be in control. Many of us felt that the private sector had had their chance. Their aim had been to create wealth for themselves.

But, it was often said that the country could "raise Hell all week", then Roosevelt would come on the radio and give one of his "fireside chats", and everyone would calm down. He would let us know everything was all right by explaining the problems and giving solutions. The people trusted what he said and did.

When I was carrying the newspaper, going from house to house, I could hear the radios and could follow the speech, house-to-house, through my whole route. When he spoke, everyone listened.

Politics was a regular subject of conversation at our house. My Mother had a political job. She worked in the Delinquent Tax Office at the Knox County Courthouse. As we grew up, we often stopped by the courthouse to see her. In the process, we would get acquainted with many of the local politicians. We soon discovered which officeholders were considered honorable and those who were considered crooked.

Because of the economic condition, many people were behind in their taxes. My Mother discovered that the elected official in her office would take some of his cronies, who owned a lot of property and were several years behind in taxes, into his office and arrange to dismiss much of the tax burden. It wasn't known whether money exchanged hands in the deal. My Mother was incensed by this activity because all the poorer people who owed back taxes had their property sold if they could not pay the total amount owed. She discovered that, according to the county law, back taxes could be dismissed if current taxes were paid. She had the County Trustee publish these facts and the percentage of back taxes to be paid in any settlement.

My Mother vowed to dismiss the taxes for every poor person, some who could not even read or write. She would help them make a reasonable settlement. She saved many poor people's farms as well as the homes of many black people in the city.

My Mother had a very strong sense of justice. It was her powerful conviction that molded my political demeanor.

CHAPTER 33

THE PAPER ROUTE

IT SEEMS AS IF MY BROTHER, Lynn, and I, as kids, always had a job, off-and-on, to make a little spending money. In the summer, we mowed grass and, at one time or another, we both carried the KNOXVILLE NEWS-SENTINEL, the evening paper, or the KNOXVILLE JOURNAL, the morning paper. When we were JOURNAL carriers, Lynn's route was Luttrell Street and the surrounding area. My route started at Central on Broadway and ended at Peters and Bradley's Mill on Bluff Street. Our paper corner was at Broadway and Central. To be sure that we were up at 3:30 a.m. we had a wind-up alarm clock that we put in a large metal pan. When the alarm kicked off, the clock would dance around in the pan, making an unavoidable sound. We were up and dressed in minutes and out the door with our paper satchel on our shoulder. It was about a ten-block walk to the paper corner, so the walk in the cool morning air tended to wake us up.

Usually, the paper bundles, secured with copper wire, had already arrived with our route numbers attached. A carrier had one or two bundles, depending on the number of customers on the route. We usually saved the copper wire for projects we had at home.

Lynn and I parted ways. We headed to the beginning of our route.

My route began with the businesses at Broad and Central. Further up Broadway, near the Broadway Baptist Church, was a distribution plant for Cedarcrest Dairy. The foreman always swapped a half-pint of chocolate milk for a paper. It was like an oasis in the early morning because there was never a more delicious drink in the early hours of the day.

Broadway was the main thoroughfare through Knoxville and was one of the most traveled streets. In the late 1930's, the street was resurfaced with a heavy coat of asphalt. I remember well when the 1100 block was resurfaced because two or three blocks of Broadway were blocked-off. The extra-smooth surface was an invitation to all of us who had skates to have a huge skating party on the new asphalt. It was wonderful to be able to skate for two or three blocks on what would be the busiest street in Knoxville.

Carrying the paper along Broadway was always exciting. The street was part of the famous Thunder Road on which bootleggers first learned to be stock car drivers. The car of choice was a 1936 Ford V8 Coupe that had an extra large trunk. When I was crisscrossing Broadway, delivering the paper, I knew when not to cross. There were sounds that signaled a fast bootlegger was coming through.

At Bluff Street, there was a creek that ran under Broadway that turned the waterwheel at Peters and Bradley's Mill. There was a wooden bridge at this point on the street. After the bridge, it was uphill for a block past a Gulf Station. Then, it was a long run uphill past the Fourth Presbyterian Church, Wright's Barber Shop, and Haliburton's Esso Station to Wells Avenue at the top of the hill. Then it leveled off.

I could hear the whine of the V8 before it came to the bridge, and I knew to wait on the curb until the car whizzed past. The speeding car would bottom-out when it crossed the wooden bridge with a "thump". Then the whine of the gears as the car started up the incline, faster and faster, until it came past me like a shot. I usually had to wait for a few minutes more because two or three Fords could be running in tandem. These V8 Fords were souped-up to the point that there was never any police pursuit. No standard car could catch them. The organization point for Thunder Road was near Cosby, Tennessee, or in the mountains of North Carolina. It ran through Knoxville on Broadway, then west out Cumberland Ave., past the University of Tennessee, on toward Chattanooga.

A friend of mine, a few years older, told me that because he had a car and was somewhat of a hot- shot driver, he was approached (after he graduated from high school) by some men asking him to drive for them. They were the good-old-boy types, and they promised him $100.00 a run, two or three runs per week, which was a fortune in the 1930's. They promised to change his license plate each run and repaint his car every third trip, bail him out of jail if he were arrested, and pay all expenses. He never took them up on their offer because he didn't want to upset his Mother.

On the dashboard of the cars, the bootleggers installed a toggle switch to turn the stop lights on and off. If, at night, they were being pursued by the police and were approaching a sharp curve, they would turn the lights off when they slowed down, hoping the police would hit the curve unaware. Then, when they were approaching a long straight-away, they would flip on the stop lights as if they were slowing down. Then, they would gun the souped-up V8 and leave the pursuit cars behind.

For young lads in the 1930's, when there was little hope, the excitement of fast cars and people escaping the clutches of the law, was a great release. They were not lawbreakers to us but heroes of the road. They were succeeding in a time when there was no success.

At the end of my route at Bluff Street, a little black woman met me everyday. She didn't want to buy a paper, she just wanted to look at it for about a minute. She raised hogs, and everyday, she wanted to check the price of pork.

Lynn and I made it back home about 6:00 a.m. as the sun began to expose above smoky Knoxville. We could rest for about an hour before we had to up and on our way to school.

So it was in the Blue Mist.

CHAPTER 34

WALKING AND RIDING

IN 1930, MY DAD SOLD OUR Studebaker auto for $100.00. The man who bought the car paid $25.00 down – the man and the car were never seen again.

From about 1930 until 1950, our family was without an automobile. We walked everywhere, individually or as a family. Downtown Knoxville was about three or four miles from our house on Eleanor Street. My elementary school, Brownlow, was only three blocks away. Park Junior High was about three miles, and Knoxville High was about two or three miles.

While going to Park Junior High, I had a "bone-tired"[2] bicycle that I rode most of the time to school. I had bought the bicycle from Robert Asqueth, a neighbor, for $6.00. When I went to high school, I was usually late. Along with the Vance brothers, we ran the distance to the school to attempt an on time arrival.

We walked to our church, First Cumberland Presbyterian, On Broadway, some three miles distance. Walking was an economic choice. It cost six cents per person for a token to ride the city bus or streetcar. Tokens were purchased five tokens for thirty cents. This

---

[2] The tires on these bicycles were called "bone-tired" because the tires were made in one piece without a removable inner tube, and the air pressure was very high to make them bone-hard.

meant if our family rode public transportation, the cost for all five of us would be thirty cents per trip. We could think of a more worthy use for this amount of money. We could buy two pounds of steak for the same sum. Food always held priority.

Sometimes, if we were Christmas shopping downtown, when the stores were open at night, we would be tired and carrying Christmas packages. On these occasions, Dad would splurge and spend the thirty cents for the family to ride the bus in style for the trip home.

Once on a rare occasion, Mother's brother, "Buck" (Elmer Burkhart), would have an auto from the car dealership where he worked as Parts Manager. I remember his coming by the church on one snowy Christmas night to pick us up after a party. It was wonderful to snuggle with the family inside the high-wheeled automobile with isinglass and canvas curtains protecting us from the cold winter wind. I never will forget the family closeness that I felt on our ride home as I listened to the crunching snow under the tires of the 1931 Studebaker.

Occasionally, we would take a short train trip to Chattanooga or to Greenville, Tennessee to visit Mother's sister, Gladys Thompson, and to Johnson City to visit her sister, Etta Wallen. Because our Daddy worked for Southern Railway, we could ride the train on a Pass without charge. Upon return to Knoxville, Daddy would meet us at the Depot. Because of the baggage, usually two small bags, we would take a taxi home. I remember, even as a child, worrying about the cost. When the taxi driver cranked on the handle of the meter, it registered thirty-five cents. Wow! That was more than the bus fare for all of us. The meter made a clicking noise as it registered the time and distance. I watched intently as the city blocks passed hoping that the meter would not register anymore cost. As we approached our house just a half-a-block away, the meter made a loud click, and the cost suddenly jumped to forty cents. My heart sank. We almost made it home for thirty-five cents, but within only a half-a-block to go, we had the cost increase to forty cents. My Dad always thought the driver had a button he pushed to increase the cost at the last minute.

CLEAR MEMORIES IN THE MIST OF TIME

Mom and Dad,

  We are sorry you grew old and died.

  You will always be young and active in our hearts.

  The glow of memories are in our soul, and we miss you.

  We can see you back in the Depression years

  To us, you were the Rock of Gibraltar

  You probably didn't feel that way, but we believed in you.

Dad,

  You were a proud man

  We never saw you in bib overalls, even though you wore them every
  work day in the railroad shop

Mother,

We don't ever remember seeing you sick

We know you were – and maybe, sick and tired

You could take a few dollars and make ends meet

You were a saint to us

Mother and Dad

You are always in our hearts

CAST OF CHARACTERS

FATHER: Darak Blackburn Armstrong

                           Born: 1895

                           Died: 1981

MOTHER: Mary Ruth (Burkhart) Armstrong

                           Born: 1899

                           Died: 1992

GRANDFATHER: John Blackburn Armstrong

                           Born 1862

                           Died:: 1949

GRANDMOTHER: Georgia Cardwell Armstrong

                           Born: 1864

                           Died: 1953

AUTHOR: Dan Cinton Armstrong, Sr., D. Min.

                           Born: 1924

BROTHER:	Lynn Blackburn Armstrong
	Born: 1926
SISTER:	Martha Ruth (Armstrong) Cooper
	Born: 1928

LOCATIONS

FIRST CUMBERLAND PRESBYTERIAN CHURCH

Broadway, Knoxville, Tennessee

The church our family and grandparents attended and were members

GAY STREET

The main street in downtown Knoxville, Tennessee

JOPPA, TENNESSEE

A small community about 30 miles from Knoxville, Tennessee, where our Grandfather owned a small farm in the mountains

1150 ELEANOR STREET

Our family's residence in north Knoxville, Tennessee

1127 ELEANOR STREET

Our Grandparents' residence about 1/2 block from our family's residence at 1150 Eleanor Street, north Knoxville, Tennessee

OAKWOOD ELEMENTARY SCHOOL

The school author Dan Armstrong attended in the second grade

BROWNLOW ELEMENTARY SCHOOL

The school author Dan Armstrong attended second grade through sixth grade

PARK JUNIOR HIGH SCHOOL

The school author Dan Armstrong attended seventh grade through ninth grade

KNOXVILLE HIGH SCHOOL

The high school author Dan Armstrong attended, graduating in 1943

ABOUT THE AUTHOR

Dr. Dan C. Armstrong is a retired Presbyterian minister (Presbyterian Church, USA). He was born June 12, 1924 in Knoxville, Tennessee and grew up during the Great Depression. The experience profoundly affected his life. Even today, he carries a profound sadness that originated in his childhood. His values and attitudes were formed by the experience as well -- the most obvious being his concern for the less fortunate of society manifesting in his actions as well his writings.

The author served as a Navy Signalman during WWII. He returned home and entered the University of Tennessee, Knoxville, graduating with a BS in Business Administration. . He is a graduate of Columbia Theological Seminary in Atlanta, Georgia. In 1980, he received his doctorate (D.Min.) from McCormick Theological Seminary in Chicago, Illinois.

After many years as a successful businessman with Smith, Kline & French Laboratories, he entered the ministry at forty years of age, graduating in 1967 from Columbia. He became pastor of Southminster Presbyterian Church, College Park, Ga, for the next twenty-five years. He then was a hospital chaplain at Emory Hospital in Atlanta, Ga., a private counselor, and Director of Social Services at the Atlanta Union Mission, a men's mission. In 1990, Dr. Armstrong was the Democrat Party nominee from Fayette County, Georgia, for the Georgia House of Representatives. In 1992, he ran for the Georgia State Senate. In 1992, Dr. Armstrong and his wife, Faith, became involved in the movie and TV business, appearing and acting in 13 major motion pictures and TV series that were being filmed in the Atlanta area at the time. They also appeared in several local TV commercials, and Dr. Armstrong appeared in a Japanese movie.

In 1993, tiring of the city, the author and his wife moved to the North Georgia mountains and a much different way of life. He continued to write and was an interim pastor for three small Presbyterian Churches. In 1999, the Armstrongs moved to Gate City, Virginia, where they now reside with an eclectic group of rescued animals on the North Fork of the Holston River, again living in the quiet of a rural setting He has retired – again – and devotes most of his time to writing, which appears in various magazines, newspapers and now this book.

5913295R0

Made in the USA
Lexington, KY
26 June 2010